HOUSE PLANTS
THROUGH THE
YEAR

Cynthia Wickham

Colour illustrations by
Julia A'Court

COLLINS

First published in 1985 by
William Collins Sons & Co. Ltd
London · Glasgow · Sydney · Auckland
Toronto · Johannesburg

© Cynthia Wickham 1985

Colour illustrations by Julia A'Court/Design Exclusive
Line illustrations by Patti Pearce/Garden Studio

Edited by Caroline Hartnell
Designed by Janet James

ISBN 0 00 410481 1

Photoset in Gill Sans by
Rowland Phototypesetting Ltd
Bury St Edmunds, Suffolk
Printed and bound in Great Britain by
Hazell Watson & Viney Ltd, Aylesbury

Contents

Introduction

Why should a book on houseplants be divided into twelve chapters, one for each month of the year?

Well, there are several reasons.

First, this book tells you about all sorts of plants you can grow in the house in addition to the traditional indoor plants. These other plants are annuals for the most part, and these have their own special timetables for sowing seed, transplanting seedlings, and so on. They cannot be bought all the year round either, so you need to know when they can be spotted for sale at the greengrocers or garden centre.

Second, even the familiar and popular indoor plants like to have a growing season and a resting season, which means they will need to be treated differently at different times of the year. Various jobs like repotting or taking cuttings are better done at some times of year than at others, so it is quite useful to have a monthly reminder about these too.

Third, for quick reference it is much easier to look up a particular month to be reminded of what you should be doing with your plants than to wade through plant descriptions to check there is nothing you have forgotten.

There *are* plant descriptions too, of course: a glossary, with illustrations of each plant to help identification, and detailed notes on the best way to look after your plants, which should enable even the beginner to keep them happy and healthy.

For every month there are quick-reference checklists of things to do, plants to buy, plants in flower, what seeds to sow, bulbs to plant, and so on. There are also step-by-step instructions on taking cuttings, sowing seed, and repotting, as well as general reference sections on subjects like compost, watering and feeding, and some of the most important sorts of plants – begonias, cacti, and ferns, to mention but a few.

Plants covered in the book

All the plants mentioned can be grown either in a room or in a window box. Some will benefit from being put outside in summer, for the maximum of fresh and refreshing baths in light showers of rain, but if this is not possible they will manage indoors with as much fresh air as you can give them and the odd shower bath from a mist-spray.

Some plants will survive adequately in ordinary rooms but would do far better in a warm greenhouse or conservatory, or in a terrarium or plant window with its own 'climate'; these are specified in the glossary. Plants which are specifically greenhouse specimens, like some of the larger climbers, are not included in this book, as it is not feasible to attempt to grow them in a house.

As I have already said, this book includes many plants which are not usually thought of as houseplants, and which you may not even realize can be grown indoors. Not many people think of tomatoes or morning glories (*ipomoea*) growing in a living room, or even an office – yet a warm, sunny windowsill can easily provide a happy home for them. Many of these 'other' plants are annuals, which can either be bought as small plantlets or sown from seed (easy to do indoors with the clean peat composts now available – houseplants, too, can be grown from seed, not just by experts in greenhouses, but by ordinary people in ordinary rooms). They will flower or fruit on a sunny windowsill or outside in a window box, and are discarded at the end of the season. Herbs are also featured, as the smaller ones make excellent houseplants – especially parsley and basil, my favourite. Finally, I include spring bulbs – how welcome they are in the very depths of winter – and the dwarf conifers and winter-flowering heathers that can give colour and interest to a window box when nothing else is about.

Some plants, like chrysanthemums, are bought in flower and then discarded, as they will not repeat their performance a second year. Others, like begonias and cyclamen, can be stored if you have the space, and brought into growth a second year. Any plants which need complicated winter cosseting, however, have been excluded.

Orchids are mentioned, as some of them can do well in rooms, though they are never the easiest houseplants in the world. Bonsai (the cultivation of miniature trees of vast age) is not, however, as these small and ancient trees are not houseplants and must spend time out of doors battling with the elements.

So this book includes more or less everything you can grow in the house – and as far as I am concerned the house extends only as far as a window box; it is not assumed that the reader has a spacious patio or balcony to fill with plants, as some so-called houseplant books seem to do, or that there is a heated conservatory within reach.

I could not live without plants, and few things in the house give me such pleasure and delight. They come in a fantastic variety of shapes and sizes, patterns and textures, colours and scents, all with their own distinct characters and personalities, and whatever your needs, there are plants that will suit you. I hope that this book will help you to find the right plants and to give them the right treatment, so that you will get as much pleasure out of them as possible.

JANUARY

January – the beginning of the year, the time for new starts and new resolutions (for a while anyway), but a bit of a dead month all the same. The excitement of Christmas is over. Outside the days may be dull and very cold: snow comes more often now than in December, and the lowest temperatures of the year can be expected in January and at the beginning of February. But, on the positive side, the days *are* getting longer, and the sun is setting later every day, and even January can astonish us with bright sunny days.

In the plant world this is the emptiest, sleepiest time of the year. In the house most of the plants are enjoying their hibernation or winter rest, but you need to look at them often to make sure they are happy. It is now that the Christmas present cyclamens and primulas, and particularly the bowls of forced spring bulbs, either bought or planted, really come into their own. The bright yellow of the daffodils, the sparkling white of the narcissi, and the soft blues and pinks of the hyacinths (not to mention their sweet, evocative scent) are a constant reminder of the inevitability of spring.

As nothing else much is happening, and there won't be a lot for you to do, you might like to try a few leaf cuttings – an African violet or a semperflorens begonia perhaps. Or you could plant a hippeastrum bulb, and almost literally watch it grow – with flowers only 4–6 weeks after planting. Finally, if you haven't ordered seeds and seedlings yet, now is the time to do so.

JANUARY

TO BUY

MANY WINTER-FLOWERING PLANTS AVAILABLE

HIPPEASTRUM BULBS, ACHIMENES AND BEGONIA TUBERS, AND SINNINGIA CORMS NOW IN SHOPS

ORDER SEEDS AND SEEDLINGS FOR PLANTING OUT IN SPRING

ORDER ORCHIDS

IN FLOWER

SPARMANNIA STARTING TO FLOWER

MANY WINTER-FLOWERING PLANTS: AZALEA, CINERARIA, CYCLAMEN, KALANCHOE, POINSETTIA, PRIMULAS, SCHLUMBERGERA AND SOLANUM

ORCHIDS IN FLOWER: COELOGYNE AND PAPHIOPEDILUM

SPRING BULBS SHOULD ALL BE FLOWERING NOW

APHELANDRA SQUARROSA AND CAPSICUMS FINISHING

OUTSIDE ERICA HEATHERS AND DWARF EVERGREENS PROVIDE THE ONLY COLOUR

1 Cissus antarctica
2 Erica
3 Miniature juniperus communis
4 Juniperus compressa
5 Iris reticulata
6 Saintpaulia
7 Philodendron scandens
8 Hyacinth
9 Saintpaulia
10 Begonia hiemalis

Looking After Your Houseplants

WATERING, FEEDING

All through the winter you must give plants only enough water to stop them drying out; plants which are obviously growing still – like some palms, which never really stop – and plants in warm rooms will need more. Cacti and succulents and overwintering geraniums, which should all be in a cool place for the winter, will be content to hibernate almost, *but not quite*, dry. Do not let plant pots stand in a saucer of water which has drained out of the pot as they will suffer from cold feet (except for cyperus and the thirsty azalea). Still no food to be given, except perhaps to some of the winter-flowering plants.

HUMIDITY

The most vital thing for most of your plants is to keep up the humidity. Even in January we sometimes get mild, damp days, and your plants will be very grateful for open windows at such times so that they can get all the fresh air possible. In warm rooms with little fresh air you must keep up the humidity round plants by mist-spraying; ferns especially need this. Spraying also helps keep the leaves clean and free of dust. Placing the pots in a larger container lined with damp peat, or standing them on trays or saucers of damp gravel or small pebbles, are other ways of keeping up the humidity they need.

POSITION

All your plants should already be in the best possible positions for the winter, but do keep checking to make sure none of your plants is too warm or too cold, in too dark a place, or in a draught. Remember to put plants on the room side of a curtained window on cold, frosty nights. If you have flowering plants in a warm living room during the day they will greatly benefit from being in a cooler place at night.

SOWING SEEDS

Probably the favourite flowering house and window box plant is the geranium (the zonal pelargonium to give it its proper name), quite rightly in my opinion as it is tough, flowers for an amazing length of time, and comes in a huge range of colours. I also love the strange smell of the leaves. These can be grown from seed, or ordered as small plants.

Seed sown in January or February should produce plants for putting out in summer. Germination takes place in 2–3 weeks at 24°C (75°F). Some of the dwarf varieties are ideal for window boxes and hanging baskets and anywhere where space is short.

Streptocarpus, the Cape primrose, has clusters of trumpet-shaped flowers in a large range of colours from white to red and deep blue. Sow the seed on the surface of the compost at 21–24°C (70–75°F), and germination should take place in 2–3 weeks. You should get flowers in the autumn, if you sow seed now. The subject of seed sowing is dealt with in more detail next month.

STARTING PLANTS INTO GROWTH

Any time from now until March you could start hippeastrum bulbs into growth; achimenes, sinningias, and tuberous-rooted begonias could also be started off about now (see p. 11 for details). And you could try planting some garlic corms. Put several in a large flowerpot in a cool, light place and hope for some sun in the summer.

ORCHIDS

Orchids are an acquired taste, and one which I must admit I have not acquired. They can have a rather sinister charm, some have pretty flowers, and some smell sweet, but so far they are not the plants for me, except glimpsed in the countryside in the grass – after all we have more than fifty wild orchids growing in the fields and hedgerows in this country. A trip to the orchid market of Bangkok might possibly change my mind, but I doubt it. But many people love them and are fascinated by them, so they must be mentioned.

In the past orchids were very much the province of the specialist with an orchid house, like the fat detective Nero Wolf in his New York apartment. Now, as the growers produce varieties which are tolerant of ordinary room conditions, they are being grown more and more as houseplants. Some are epiphytes growing in trees, some are terrestrial, or ground-growing; the latter are usually the ones to be sold for the house.

Since orchids are a plant family on their own, and a very complicated one, and since they require a great deal more care than many of the more common houseplants, it is always best to buy from specialist nurseries, which will be able to give you advice as to how to keep them happy, and to pay the rather high prices they ask. As they are ordered in the winter, to be dispatched in March or April, you could still get some if you order now. Those which you order by post come with detailed instructions on their care, and they will be alright in the pots they come in for 2 years before repotting. One thing to remember about orchids is that they all need a high degree of humidity and hate a dry atmosphere.

Some of the easiest are covered in the Glossary: coelogyne, miltonia and paphiopedilum. Others you might try are cymbidium, dendrobium, lycaste, odontoglossum, and oncidium. All these have been specially bred to withstand normal house conditions.

TAKING CUTTINGS

If you can be sure of keeping them warm and with sufficient humidity, you could take leaf cuttings of African violets, cissus, and small-leaved begonias and peperomias now (see p. 10). You can in fact do this at any time of year, but now seems a good time as you will not be so busy doing other things like sowing seeds, or repotting.

PROPAGATION TIPS

Seeds
Last chance to order from seed catalogues; streptocarpus and geraniums could be sown early.

Cuttings
Leaf cuttings and stem cuttings of some particularly easy plants can be taken any time.

Bulbs
Achimenes, hippeastrum, sinningia, tuberous-rooted begonias could be started into growth.

Plants to Buy

At this time of year there is quite a large selection of flowering houseplants to choose from. The two I would always have if possible are white or pale pink cyclamen and blue and white hyacinths. Primulas are another great favourite of mine, for they are both long-lasting and pretty. Other winter plants I particularly like are poinsettias, azaleas and cinerarias. Saintpaulias (African violets) are almost always available, and for those who can keep them they are a constant source of joy. I must admit here that I cannot, and they are not among my favourites.

The huge hippeastrum bulbs are around in the shops, and achimenes and begonia tubers and sinningia corms, as you can start them into growth any time now (see p. 11). If you have a window box or other container outside you might consider planting some small evergreen conifers, like the pretty little cypresses, junipers and yews (see p. 85 for suggestions).

If you are buying plants do be careful not to let them get too cold on the way from the nursery or shop – particularly those that require a lot of warmth, and particularly if the weather is very cold. Take them straight home, rather than leaving them for hours in the car in freezing conditions.

LOOKING AFTER THESE FLOWERING PLANTS

Many plants bought at this time of year are doomed, as they miss the greenhouse atmosphere and the humidity. Frequent spraying, a cool place, and either putting moist pebbles beneath the flower pot or placing the pot in a larger one, packed round with damp peat, will help lengthen their lives. Both cyclamen and *Primula*

malacoides will do best in a cool place with the pot on a saucer of damp gravel; in these conditions they will flower a long time. You can also give them a little fertilizer once a week.

Azalea indica often arrives smothered in flowers and then proceeds to drop them all. It is usually pot-bound and extremely thirsty – in fact it is one of the few plants that can safely be left with water in its saucer. As with the other flowering plants it will help to put it in a cooler place at night if it is gracing the warm living room during the day. These

cannot be kept for another year so must be given to a friend with a greenhouse, or someone who can put the whole pot outside in the garden for the summer and bring it in before the frosts, whereupon it will flower again the next winter, although probably less profusely.

Poinsettias should be cut down when the coloured bracts fade and repotted in May; they should then be put outside in the earth for the summer, so for the gardenless they, too, are purely temporary houseplants, and none the worse for that as they do last a long time.

TAKING LEAF CUTTINGS

Although the best time for taking cuttings of plants to root them is August (see pp. 70–71), leaf cuttings of saintpaulia (African violet), cissus, and small-leaved begonias and peperomias can be rooted at any time of year. The temperature should not be lower than 18°C (64°F). Young leaves with about 5 cm (2 in) of stem can be removed from the parent plant and put 2.5 cm (1 in) deep in a mixture of sand and peat so that the leaf is above the surface. Soon small plants will form at the base of the leaves; these can be potted individually into small pots when large enough. To be certain of the temperature you may consider a small heated propaga-

tor, but it is perfectly possible to do this in a room if you cover the pot with a plastic bag held up with canes to conserve the humidity round the cuttings. Or you can use one of those clear plastic domes sold in plant shops. It also helps to dip the ends of the stems into a rooting powder before inserting them into the compost.

This is a good way to build up a collection of plants, and plants grown from cuttings always mean something special. If you acquired the cutting from a friend, the plant will always remind you of that friend, and of the occasion when you took the cutting.

Leaf cuttings of African violets

ORDERING SEEDS AND SEEDLINGS

There are many plants other than the traditional houseplants which can be grown in houses, and many of these can be grown from seed. It is well worth while getting hold of the catalogues of good seedsmen. November and December are the best times to order seeds but you can still do so now.

Obviously it all depends on what space and time you have to spare. I love to grow seeds on a window sill in the warmth, to prick them out and pot them on. On the other hand, I can see that it is too much of a bother for many people.

There are different levels of seed sowing, too. Some plants like tomatoes and morning glory are easy to raise, but some – those of the perennial houseplants, for example – will need cosseting at a particular temperature, and for this you will very likely need a heated propagator.

I find it so rewarding to raise one or two plants from seed, and a tomato or green pepper plant is a most decorative thing. (Some of the specially small tomato plants suitable for window boxes and pots are hard to find in the shops and therefore best grown from seed.) You may well be amazed, however, at the number of houseplants which can be grown from seed, germinating quite quickly and growing fast. I know of a banana palm in London which is over 3.5 m (11 ft) tall and grown from a seed 3 years ago. I myself have a mysterious Antipodean tree which grew from a large bean a friend gave me 2 years ago. It sat in its pot of compost for months and I was about to give it up when I noticed a huge mass of roots and a tiny shoot. This sort of thing can give you so much pleasure. My favourite sage plant started life on a bathroom sill. With plants the price they are it makes quite a saving to grow from seed, and if you end up with a regular small forest then the plants make lovely presents.

In the last few years seedsmen have been offering not only seeds but seedlings and young plants too. These are mainly

STARTING PLANTS INTO GROWTH

HIPPEASTRUM (AMARYLLIS)

A plant I would not like to be without at the beginning of the year is the hippeastrum. This is surely one of the fastest growers of all plants as the large bulbs, started into growth by watering and warmth, can be brought into flower in as little as 4 weeks. The lily-shaped trumpet flowers are large and dramatic, in scarlet, crimson and shades of pink and cream, and never fail to cause a stir. I love them. There is a cottage next to a grocer's shop in our local small town where one of the great spring treats for passers-by is to gaze in at the window where four or five of these theatrical flowers share the small window with spring bulbs, and a fluffy white cat – an unforgettable picture. How lucky for us all that the old lady who grows them realizes that plants in a window on the street not only give her pleasure but everybody who goes by as well. A Dutch friend of mine says that in Holland blinds and curtains are kept to a minimum so that strollers can see in, not only to notice how impeccably clean the rooms are, but also to admire the plants in the windows.

These plants are spring- or early summer-flowering in nature but readily available now. The large, firm bulbs must be put into a 15 cm (6 in) pot filled with a good compost, the top half of the bulb being left uncovered. Put them somewhere at a temperature of 16–21°C (61–70°F), and start watering when you see the beginnings of growth. Stems reach on average 45–60 cm (18–24 in). The plant must be kept warm and watered regularly until the strap-like leaves have stopped growing; round about September or October it should be put in the cool to dry out and rest before being started into growth again next winter or spring. You only have to repot every 3 years but the top 2.5 cm (1 in) of compost should be replaced with fresh every year (this is known as top-dressing).

ACHIMENES

Achimenes are staging a bit of a comeback; they were popular Victorian plants, and known as the hot water plant in the parlours of those days. The flowers appear in summer, in all shades of red, pink, purple and white, and covering the plants. The tiny tubers or rhizomes can be started into growth at any time from January to March; plant them 2 cm (¾ in) deep in a peat compost at about 16–21°C (61–70°F) in a shady place. When sprouts show they can be put into a brighter light. Give them a light, airy place and a fortnightly feed and dead-head regularly and they will flower all summer.

SINNINGIAS

Sinningias, or gloxinias as they used to be called, are beautiful summer-flowering pot-plants, with velvety leaves and bell-shaped flowers of enormous size and vivid colours. The corms of these plants are in the shops from January to March and may be started into growth any time from late January. Put the corms singly in 10–13 cm (4–5 in) pots in peaty compost with the tops of the dried tubers just level with the surface. Keep them at a temperature round about 21°C (70°F), and put the pots in a dark plastic bag to conserve moisture until shoots appear. Normal room temperatures suit these plants; 16°C (61°F) is ideal for healthy growth. At the end of the season the leaves will turn yellow and wither; they should then be removed, the pots allowed to dry out, and the tubers stored in dry peat over the winter.

TUBEROUS-ROOTED BEGONIAS

These are some of the most dazzling plants, flowering from May to November, and these, like sinningias, are started into growth between late January and March. Put the tubers into 13–15 cm (5–6 in) pots, one to a pot, hollow side up, just covered with soil, at 13–18°C (55–64°F); water moderately until growth begins.

for the outdoor gardener but can also be useful for the window box owner. Some are sold in batches of a hundred, which is no good unless you can share with friends, but you can also order packs of ten, and for people who have neither the time nor the inclination to grow from seed these are ideal. You can grow them on with none of the bother of seeds, seed compost and propagators, and they are guaranteed strong and healthy as they have been grown in the best possible conditions.

All the large seedsmen supply these plants – geraniums, begonias and fuchsias, tomatoes, aubergines and green peppers.

They should be ordered in the winter, and all will be delivered in time for planting outside, in window boxes or containers, or in pots on sunny, airy sills, in April or May.

Some orchids can be grown as houseplants. If you want to try one or two now is a good time to order them (see p. 9).

SPROUTING SEEDS TO EAT

Sprouting seeds have become a popular part of healthy diets, and it is certainly very pleasing to produce fresh, crunchy vegetables full of vitamins in only 3–6 days from seed, at any time of year and regardless of good or bad weather. They are surely ideal food plants to grow in the house. As you will need a lot of these seeds many of them are supplied in 450 g (1 lb) plastic tubs.

Alfalfa has a taste reminiscent of garden peas; *bean shoots or mung beans*, and *salad sprouts* are both ideal for salads and sandwiches. Mung beans can be grown on wet tissues and are ready for your Chinese meals in 6–9 days; alfalfa, grown in a glass jar, produces green shoots in 5–7 days, as do *alphatoco* sprouts and *fenugreek*, all full of vitamins and minerals. They come with instructions, and all you need to grow them is a coffee jar and a piece of muslin

or tissue. If you do not want to eat them at once the sprouted seeds can be put in sealed plastic bags in a freezer and will keep crisp for 3 weeks.

The homely *mustard and cress* must not be forgotten when thinking of food plants to grow in the house, since they too can be grown at any time and their fresh, green taste of summer sandwiches is particularly welcome in winter. They are also, of course, full of vitamins.

The ultimate food plant for the house is the *mushroom*, and these can be grown in special compost from spawn, usually in a bucket. They will grow in a dark or semi-dark place with a temperature of 10–15°C (50–59°C), and you could be picking mushrooms in 6–8 weeks from sowing the spawn. You can eat them button size or let them grow, and more will keep coming over a further 6–8 weeks.

FEBRUARY

Being an incurable optimist, I always think that spring begins this month, although it *can* be the worst month of the year and we may be up to our noses in snow. However, looking on the bright side, February is good because it has St Valentine's Day, traditionally the birds' wedding day. It is also the birthday month of the snowdrops, the fair maids of February, often standing in the snow. Sensible souls who have bought bulbs in the autumn can also have these beauties in bowls in the house or in window boxes. The enchanting little yellow aconites with their green ruffs also appear this month, telling us that this is the end of the winter. People say that if the wind is in the east at the beginning of the month then winter is with us for another 4 or 5 weeks, but if the wind is in the west, bringing clouds and rain, then we must prepare for an early spring. This month is called February fill dyke in some parts of the country because of the rain – and flooding – it all too often brings.

Most of the houseplants will still be dormant so there will not be a great deal for the indoor gardener to do. Towards the end of the month, however, some of the plants will begin to wake up, and you will need to tidy them up, perhaps move them to a different position, and begin to give more water. About now, also, you can start sowing seeds of the annual flowers, vegetables and herbs that will grow on your window sills and outside in boxes and containers later in the year. It may still feel like the depths of winter, but it is now that you have to start preparing for the summer that is on its way.

FEBRUARY

TO BUY

MANY WINTER-FLOWERING PLANTS STILL AVAILABLE

BUY PRIMROSES AND POLYANTHUS TO REPLACE WINTER-FLOWERING PLANTS AS THEY FINISH

HIPPEASTRUM BULBS, ACHIMENES AND BEGONIA TUBERS, AND SINNINGIA CORMS

NEW POTS AND COMPOST FOR REPOTTING

LAST CHANCE TO ORDER SEEDS AND SEEDLINGS

IN FLOWER

CLIVIA AND HIPPEASTRUM STARTING TO FLOWER

STILL MANY WINTER-FLOWERING PLANTS: AZALEA, CINERARIA, CYCLAMEN, KALANCHOE, POINSETTIA, PRIMULAS AND SCHLUMBERGERA

COELOGYNE, PAPHIOPEDILUM, JASMINE AND SPARMANNIA STILL FLOWERING

SPRING BULBS STILL FLOWERING

OUTSIDE WINTER ACONITE, SNOWDROPS AND CROCUSES WILL BE APPEARING ALONGSIDE THE ERICA HEATHERS

1	Fatshedera lizei
2	Tradescantia fluminensis
3	Narcissus
4	Spathiphyllum
5	Snowdrop
6	Zebrina pendula

Looking After Your Houseplants

WATERING, FEEDING

Still a quiet time for the houseplants, with nothing much to be done. Basically the same rules apply as for January. Keep an eye on your plants, and make sure they are just moist, not overwatered. And still no food to be given.

Towards the end of the month, as you move overwintering plants – geraniums, cacti and succulents, fuchsias, hydrangeas – to sunnier positions (see below), you should start giving them gradually more water (for cacti and succulents their first drink of the year, apart from the odd drop given to prevent their compost drying out completely).

HUMIDITY

Give your plants the benefit of fresh air on clement days, and keep up the moisture round plants in warm, dry rooms by mist-spraying and by standing the pots on damp pebbles or gravel or in containers of moist peat. Don't forget that all flowering houseplants will bloom much longer if they are in a cool, bright place, and will greatly appreciate a mist-spray every now and then to keep them fresh. Fuchsias that are just starting into growth will appreciate frequent spraying.

POSITION

As the days get lighter and, we hope, sunnier towards the end of the month, overwintering plants such as geraniums, fuchsias, hydrangeas, cacti and succulents may be moved into brighter, warmer positions. Fuchsias will appreciate a place in the morning sun, if this is possible.

SPECIAL MIXTURES

Certain plants like orchids need special mixtures, which should be used if you get to the stage of repotting these plants. For epiphytic orchids that will often be a bark-based compost with peat and sphagnum moss, while terrestrial (ground-growing) orchids are often sold in an equal mix of bark, loam, sand, sphagnum moss and leaf mould or moss peat. There are ready-mixed composts available, and your supplier will be able to advise you which to use.

There are also special mixtures available for bromeliads, cacti, heathers and ferns, but these should not be necessary; I have always managed with ordinary compost. Flowering bulbs for the winter can be grown in a special bulb fibre mixture, but an ordinary peat compost will do quite well.

For the most part all you are likely to need for an average plant collection is a bag of peat-based compost, a bag of loam-based (John Innes No. 2), and a bag of some sort of grit. Any new plant in its plastic pot will almost certainly be in a peat-based compost, and this will have enough nourishment in it to keep the plant happy for 6 months before you have to think about feeding it. Fertilizers are dealt with in the March chapter (see p. 28).

You can sow houseplant seeds any time from February to May or June, provided you can be sure of the right temperatures. Late spring is probably the best time of all, except for monstera which should ideally be sown in May or June. See p. 43 for some suggestions as to what seeds you might try. You can either order these from seedsmen or look out for them in the shops.

STARTING PLANTS INTO GROWTH

Hippeastrum bulbs, achimenes and begonia tubers, and sinningia (gloxinia) corms can be started into growth in a warm place any time from January to March (see p. 11).

As it is garlic planting time outside you could put some corms into a large flower pot in a cool, light place. If they get sun in the summer you may well get useful heads in July.

KEEPING THE LEAVES CLEAN, PRUNING

As always make sure the leaves of your plants are always clean and free of dust. Most plants can be given a shower bath in the bath, or their leaves can be wiped (this is important as plants transpire through their leaves). Cacti need to be dry, however, particularly in the cold weather, and must be kept dust-free with a soft brush.

Geraniums, fuchsias and hydrangeas will all need a light prune and general tidy-up.

TOP-DRESSING

At the end of the month you could top-dress the soil in large pots with well-established plants in them – hydrangeas, bay, heptapleurum and sparmannia, for example. This means removing the top 5–8 cm (2–3 in) of the soil and replacing with fresh compost. This can be done any time between now and the end of April.

SOWING SEEDS

Houseplants are expensive, and recently more and more seedsmen have been including seeds in their lists, so that people can raise their own. Some of these can be successfully germinated in a house as long as the temperature is right – another use for a heated propagator. Naturally these are not as easy as ordinary bedding plants or vegetables to raise from seed, but they are well worth trying; most of the seedlings will grow to a great height and be happy in the house for years.

PROPAGATION TIPS

Seeds
First month for sowing most houseplant seeds (see p. 43 for suggestions); first sowings of annuals like tomatoes, aubergines, peppers, chillies, herbs.

Cuttings
Could take leaf cuttings and stem cuttings of particularly easy plants.

Bulbs
Achimenes, hippeastrum, sinningia, tuberous-rooted begonias, garlic, and reichsteineria (cardinal flower) can be started into growth.

AS PLANTS DIE DOWN

Cyclamen, which have done so much to brighten the winter, may well be dying down now (though they could last a month longer), as will the solanums (winter cherry). If you want to keep the cyclamen, gently remove the foliage, and keep the corm dry until next August.

Solanums are usually discarded in spring when they have finished. It is possible to keep them but only if you have somewhere outside where they can go in spring and summer, in which case they should be potted on, the stems cut back by half, watered and fed. Later you will need to pinch them out to encourage bushiness, spray them when budding to encourage fruits, and bring them indoors in September to begin all over again. A bit of a performance and impossible without some outside space, so perhaps it's better to enjoy them and then throw them out, and buy new next autumn. You could replace the cyclamen and solanums with small primroses and polyanthus.

Annuals and Outdoor Plants

FOOD PLANTS

As a general rule most seeds are sown in March and April, but some benefit from an early start, provided you can be sure of the warmth they need. Amongst these are some of the food plants which can be grown in the house or in boxes outside.

The tomato, or 'love apple' as it was first called, was in fact first grown as a purely decorative plant, and the fruits were considered strange to eat, if not positively dangerous. Tomato seeds are sown in February or March at a temperature of 18–21°C (64–70°F). The seedlings are then pricked out and put singly into 5 or 8 cm (2 or 3 in) pots of potting compost to grow on until planted out into their final pot, tub or gro-bag. Plants do well on a sunny window sill as long as

they are given enough water and fertilizer: tomatoes are very thirsty and hungry as they are so quick-growing. Outside they must have a warm, sunny place. Plants cannot be put outside until there is no danger of frost, early June in the north and May in the south. Being quick-growing they like John Innes No.3, but they also do splendidly in the peat composts. It is best to stick to the smaller varieties for indoor or window box growing, though for a gro-bag outside, on a flat roof for instance, any of the usual varieties can be planted, three to a bag.

The smaller gro-bags can sit on a wide sill inside, or on a sheltered window ledge outside. They can be used for all sorts of flowers and vegetables as well as the traditional tomatoes. You could grow lettuces, spinach, tomatoes, sweet peppers, aubergines, chillies, French beans, pansies, polyanthus, small sweetpeas, begonias or strawberries in these bags.

Aubergine (eggplant) is a warm-weather vegetable, ideal for growing outside on a sunny, sheltered window ledge, or indoors by a light window. Seeds are usually sown in April, but in the right conditions these, too, can be sown as early as February. With regular watering, feeding and sunshine, they should bear fruit in 70–90 days, and all the time they are decorative plants.

Capsicums (sweet peppers) are also pretty plants. Sow seeds this month and next at 18–21°C (64–70°F), prick out into single pots, and plant out in May or June. Chillies, with their fiery red fruits for curries and sambals, are grown in the same way. (See p. 19 for general tips on sowing seed.)

HERBS

Seeds can also be sown around now. See pp. 46–47 for suggestions as to what herbs you might grow.

FOOD PLANTS

A number of the annual food plants make very good pot plants, both inside and out; they look decorative, and it is great fun seeing how many tomatoes or sweet peppers you can produce. Those to try are tomatoes, sweet peppers, chillies, aubergines, and dwarf climbing beans. Of course they will do better in a greenhouse or conservatory, but if you have neither of these then a sunny kitchen or office window sill will do well, as will a window box or gro-bag outside.

For one or two plants it is best to buy them small in April or May and plant them into larger pots, placing them in the sunniest, airiest place you can find. With all

food plants it is important to remember that they grow non-stop at terrific speed and will need daily watering and weekly feeding. You can of course grow them from seed if you prefer, but it is a more complicated business, as seeds go in early, especially for tomatoes, and need to be warm. Also with seeds you always get far more than you need. Some of the seedsmen supply small-scale plants bred specifically for window boxes or gro-bags; tomatoes, especially, can grow very tall and will need the support of canes or string. (See above for when and how to sow seed.)

SOWING SEED

The earliest time for sowing seeds is this month, and next is the busiest of all.

Seed sowing is only one way of propagating plants; the other main way is by taking cuttings, which are then rooted. This is dealt with in the August chapter.

Seed sowing needs a little more perseverance and patience than propagation from cuttings because you are starting right at the beginning. Growing from seed is sometimes the only way to get a special plant which you cannot find in the shops or which costs a fortune; it is also enormously satisfying and an inexpensive way of producing plants to give away as presents.

A plastic dome or lid with ventilation holes is really best. Do not let the compost dry out. Check the boxes every day, and as soon as the little seedlings appear remove the cover and put the box in a light place. Protect the box from strong sun and turn it daily or all the seedlings will grow towards the light.

WHAT YOU WILL NEED

You can raise most seeds in an ordinary seed tray, preferably with a clear plastic lid to conserve humidity like a miniature greenhouse. All you need is a warm place. With some seeds the temperature is vital, and in this case you might consider a small heated propagator or base. A propagator base is a flat, heated metal slab large enough for two seed trays; it can be placed anywhere. There will be a thermostat to prevent the temperature going too high, and it will be insulated. The most common size is 45 × 38 cm (18 × 15 in), 220–240 volt, AC 24 watt.

You can also buy small propagators very cheaply. These consist of a seed box with heater and plastic cover, and the smallest measures 35 × 23 cm (14 × 9 in), but there are other sizes to choose from. One useful piece of equipment is a self-watering propagator set which can be hooked over a domestic radiator to use its 'free' heat to germinate the seeds.

If all this is too complicated and expensive for the small amount of seed sowing or rooting from cuttings you expect to do then all you will need is a seed tray or two and an ordinary room thermometer.

WHAT TO DO

Always buy your seeds from a reputable seedsman; the packet will give you instructions about how, when and where to sow, but here are some general rules.

SOWING THE SEED
The two essentials are moisture and warmth. Sow seeds which are large enough to handle in seed compost in a box or pot 1.5–4 cm (½–1½ in) apart;

very small seed is scattered on the surface of the soil, which is gently pressed flat. Larger seeds are usually covered with a depth of soil more or less equal to their diameter. Sow in seed trays, pots, or even empty plastic cartons. Whatever container you use must have drainage holes as soggy soil will kill seedlings, so don't forget to make a hole in the base of a plastic carton before you put in the compost.

For sowing large seeds the little Jiffy pots are ideal – you don't have to cope with seed compost or trays; just soak the compressed blocks in a bowl of water to swell them up and then sow one to three seeds in the centre of each 'pot'. When the seedlings appear you keep the best and strongest from each pot and discard the others, putting the young plants attached to the Jiffy in a pot of compost when they are large enough.

After the seeds are sown (evenly and not too thickly; you never need as many as you think you do, so save some for next year) the containers must be watered, either with the fine rose of a watering can from above or by immersing the container in water to just below the rim until the compost looks damp at the top. Then drain.

Needless to say the compost must be fresh sterilized soil or you will have all sorts of strange and unwanted young plants popping up from weed seed in the mixture.

Light is not important for germination, just moisture and warmth, so any warm place – a warm cupboard or a sill or shelf above a heater – will do. The seed tray should be covered with a plastic lid or sheet of glass, or, failing this, enclosed in a clear plastic bag, to keep in the moisture.

PRICKING OUT
The first leaves to develop will be the seed leaves or cotyledons. These are either single like grass or in pairs and rounded. The second pair of leaves will be the true leaves. When these appear, or just after, it is time to 'prick out' (carefully remove) the tiny seedlings, separate them, and put them in new containers or boxes so that they can grow on ready for the final planting. The small seedlings must be removed with as little root disturbance as possible; that is why they are pricked out and replanted at an early stage. They grow so fast that the little roots soon become entangled and can get damaged when they are separated.

To separate the seedlings you can lift out a bunch with a trowel or large spoon, or shake the whole boxful on to a piece of newspaper, and shake gently, or tease them apart, always remembering to hold the leaves and not the roots. Put them in potting compost in their new container or pot, in holes made with a pencil or stick 2.5–5 cm (1–2 in) apart. Tuck them in very gently, and leave them to grow on in a light place until they are touching each other and growing strongly. Then it is time to pot them on into their larger pots or boxes. Keep the compost moist, don't let it dry out, and don't overwater. In most cases they will be ready for planting out, if they are to go outside, by the time the danger of frost is past.

COMPOSTS

Since February is really the beginning of seed sowing time it seems a good place to talk about soil and compost mixtures.

The compost in which a plant grows is vital to its health; any old garden soil will not do as it may well contain all manner of pests, grubs or trace elements. For all pot and container gardening it is important to buy reputable brands. These come in two types: loam- (ordinary top soil) based, and peat-based (so-called soilless).

LOAM COMPOSTS

The best-known loam composts are the John Innes mixtures. These mixtures were developed in the 1930s, and the formulas are made up by various manufacturers. They are a combination of loam, peat, sand and fertilizers, and come in three grades – John Innes Nos. 1, 2, and 3. The numbers indicate how much fertilizer is added. No. 1 is generally used for seedlings and young plants growing in small pots, No. 2 for established plants and as a good general-purpose mix for window boxes, etc., and No. 3, with three times as much fertilizer as No. 1, for quick growers like tomatoes in large pots. There is also a John Innes seed compost. All these are available in various sized bags, from handy packs to large. They are particularly good for cacti, succulents and geraniums.

PEAT COMPOSTS

As good loam from the meadows got scarcer and scarcer, and because it is rather heavy, peat-based composts were developed in the late 1950s; now almost every new houseplant is set in a peat mixture. These loamless composts are sometimes mixed with sand, and have added fertilizers. Peat has no food value in itself, but contains humus-forming salts which enable it to take in fertilizers and store them for the plant. It can also hold a good deal of water without becoming waterlogged, and allows a good supply of air to get to the plant roots. The big advantage peat composts have over loam is lightness: bags weigh much less and pots filled with them are easy to lift and move. This can be a drawback when tall plants become top-heavy and fall over, but if the pot is the right size and the compost damp enough this should not happen.

Peat compost must be loose in the pot, just shaken down and not rammed in tight, and it *must be kept moist*. It did at first present some watering problems to people used to old-fashioned loam, as the pots need watering less frequently. If it is allowed to dry out, on the other hand, it shrinks and leaves a space round the sides of the pot so that the water just falls straight through; the remedy for this is to stand the pot in a bucket of water for an hour or so.

When they are damp these peat composts dry out very slowly, so they are perfect for plants that need a continuously moist habitat – ferns and jungle plants, for example.

ADDING GRIT OR HUMUS TO YOUR COMPOST

Most plants are happy in peat-based composts except the sun-lovers like cacti, succulents and geraniums. But if the mixture becomes boggy and waterlogged as a result of overwatering – as alas it can – this is bad news for the plant, particularly if the temperature is low. This is why it is often suggested that you add grit or sand or Perlite (plastic grit in little balls) to these composts to 'open up' the mixture, creating more air pockets and ensuring that the water drains away easily.

Some of the peat composts have sand in them already – the information on the bag will tell you. If not you can make a mixture yourself, using 3 parts peat to one of sand, grit or Perlite. It is worth mentioning here that the grit should be granite or flint (not lime), and that it must be washed and not dusty – don't get any old builder's grit and put it in. The chips should be fine, with a maximum diameter of 3 mm (⅛ in), and jagged-edged.

Humus, which is made naturally in the wild through the decay of leaves and other vegetable matter, produces the nutrients which we have to supply in the form of plant food. Leaf mould is sometimes added to the soil to condition it and to maintain fertility; this, too, can be bought in plastic bags.

Plants to Buy

Although it is almost the beginning of spring this can be a cold and depressing time, but there are plenty of plants about to cheer these last grey days of winter. Cyclamen are still flowering in the house and in the shops – they are among the most beautiful of flowers, the petals turned back as though they have their faces into the wind. Cinerarias are still about, neat plants, and long-lasting, with pretty daisy-shaped flowers, and so are the primulas. Although it is getting rather late for these, you might still find an azalea, or schlumbergera, the Christmas cactus, with its bright flowers at the end of the flattened stems. You might also find *Clivia miniata*, though these will probably be more in evidence next month.

Or you could always buy a hippeastrum bulb and be amazed at the speed with which the tall stem and exotic flowers appear – only 4–6 weeks from the time of planting. Achimenes and begonia tubers and sinningia corms will also be available now.

If you are buying houseplants this month – flowering ones or a foliage plant – the only thing to remember is not to let them get too cold on the way back from the shop or nursery, particularly if you buy a plant that is susceptible to low temperatures.

On the more strictly practical level, with the main sowing and potting time to come in the next couple of months, you should be thinking now about buying new pots, containers and compost.

MARCH

Wonderful March, my favourite month. It can have the most varied weather from day to day, be freezing one year and get us all out into the sun with our sun tan cream the next. Whatever the weather is like, it is now that spring arrives in the south (in the north this happens in April). The clocks go forward, the hours of sunshine get longer, the sun is warmer; in sheltered places and on window sills cats, people and plants bask in its warmth. Who cares if there is a bit of snow? After all, we can still get that in April and May.

Out in the garden the preparation and digging begin, seed packets are in all the shops, and even gardeners with only a window sill get caught up in the general excitement – for March and April are the most exciting months in the gardening year, when everything starts to happen.

The houseplants will really be waking up now, so you will need to tidy them up, give them gradually more water, and start feeding. Many will want to be moved, either into the sun or away from it. You could also start thinking about repotting, a major task at this time of year. This is also the time when seed sowing begins in earnest – though if you sowed seed last month you may already have little seedlings ready to be pricked out.

MARCH

TO BUY

BOWLS OF MIXED PLANTS FOR MOTHERS' DAY

CLIVIA MINIATA

HIPPEASTRUM BULBS, ACHIMENES AND BEGONIA TUBERS, AND SINNINGIA CORMS

COMPOST, FERTILIZER, SAND, GRIT, CANES, WIRE, SEED TRAYS, POTS, ETC., FOR THE SUMMER

ORDER DWARF CONIFERS AND HEATHERS FOR WINDOW BOXES FOR NEXT WINTER

IN FLOWER

ALOES, RHIPSALIDOPSIS AND ZANTEDESCHIA STARTING TO FLOWER

CINERARIA, CLIVIA, HIPPEASTRUM, JASMINE, KALANCHOE, PAPHIOPEDILUM AND PRIMULAS STILL FLOWERING

SPARMANNIA, SPRING BULBS AND WINTER-FLOWERING PLANTS LIKE CYCLAMEN AND POINSETTIA COMING TO AN END

OUTSIDE ERICAS WILL BE NEARLY OVER BUT MANY MORE SPRING BULBS FLOWERING

1	Hedera helix
2	Daffodils
3	Cineraria
4	Ficus benjamina
5	Chionodoxa
6	Aconite
7	Primrose
8	Scindapsus

Looking After Your Houseplants

WATERING

This is the true beginning of spring, the time of year when most houseplants start growing again after their winter rest, so you will need to give your plants gradually increasing amounts of water. Apart from an odd drop during the winter, to prevent the compost completely drying out, and perhaps a little more at the end of February, the cacti and succulents will have been almost without water until now.

FEEDING

With the warmth and light (see below, under Position) and water growth should be dramatic. Once growth is really evident you should start giving fertilizer, which should then be given weekly or fortnightly until August or September. But it is important only to give it when the plant is obviously bursting into life, never when the compost is dry, or when the plant is static. And at risk of boring repetition it must be stressed that the instructions on the fertilizer pack must always be kept to. Always give a little less rather than too much, thinking (mistakenly) to give the plant a treat.

HUMIDITY

As in January and February, open windows on mild days, and remember to keep up humidity round plants in warm, dry rooms. Ferns, arums and other plants that like humid conditions will be particularly grateful for this.

LILIES AS HOUSEPLANTS

Lilies in pots in rooms have a romantic, Pre-Raphaelite air, and are worth considering even if they do not repeat their flowering performance another year. Ideally, they should be planted outside in the garden in the late summer if you want them to flower again, but you can repot them in fresh compost once the stems have died down if you want to try them indoors for a second year. The bulbs are not cheap, but then neither are a number of other temporary flowering houseplants – like the primulas in the winter, for instance – and when you compare the cost with that of a splendid bunch of cut flowers, and compare the length of time you will get pleasure from them, then they seem amazingly good value. Or so I think.

Lilies in pots like a loam-based compost, though they will grow quite well in a peat one. John Innes No. 1 suits them, with half to an equal amount of moist peat mixed in. Clay pots are best, with a good layer of broken crocks at the bottom for drainage.

A 15 cm (6 in) pot will hold three small bulbs (like *Lilium pumilum*), or one medium bulb ('Enchantment', for instance). A 20 cm (8 in) pot will hold three medium bulbs or one large one (*L. auratum*, for example). Cover the drainage layer of crocks with compost and place the bulbs low in the pot so that at least 10 cm (4 in) of compost covers them. Put the pots in a darkish place and keep them moist and cool, not above 10°C (50°F) immediately after planting; when shoots are 8 cm (3 in) high move pots to a lighter place but keep cool. When buds form on the stems plants should be at a temperature of 18–21°C (64–70°F) if possible, and they should be fed weekly with a dilute feed or fortnightly with full-strength. Plant bulbs in March or April for flowers in June or July. You should get flowers about 6 weeks after the buds appear. You can also buy specially treated bulbs to flower in February or March.

There are two main types suitable for pots. First there are the Asiatic hybrids, which flower in June:

'*Connecticut King*', 75 cm (2½ ft), with yellow star flowers;
'*Enchantment*', 60–90 cm (2–3 ft), with vivid orange curved petals, and
'*Pirate*', 60–75 cm (2–2½ ft), with red-orange flowers and dark foliage.

Then there are the trumpet types, flowering in July and August:

'*L. regale*', 1 m (3 ft), with pink-maroon buds and white trumpets spotted with gold and purple on the reverse;
'*Pink Perfection*', 75–90 cm (2½–3 ft), with scented pink trumpets, and
'*Golden Splendor*', 1 m (3 ft), with yellow trumpets.

POSITION

Most houseplants should now be put into brighter, sunnier positions. If you haven't already done so move your geraniums from their retiring, cool winter positions and put them in a bright, warm place; the same applies to the little hibernating cacti.

Although most of your plants will need to be moved to brighter, sunnier positions, delicate plants and those in flower may well be better moved, if possible, from south-facing to west-facing windows as the days get warmer.

KEEPING THE LEAVES CLEAN

Keep all leaves free of dust, by wiping or spraying or brushing with a soft brush. Some of your plants may need to be tidied up, and have dead leaves removed.

REPOTTING AND POTTING ON

March and April are the main months for potting on and repotting (see p. 35), so you should look at the root ball of your plants and see if they need a more spacious home. You may need to lay in some larger pots.

TOP-DRESSING

Any well-established plants in large pots outside or in hallways will do much better if the top 5–8 cm (2–3 in) of soil are removed and replaced with fresh compost – I am thinking of plants like hydrangeas or formal bay trees on balconies or front door steps. Do this now or next month if you haven't already done so.

SOWING SEEDS

This is another month when you could try sowing some houseplant seeds, as long as you can be sure of the temperatures they need for germination. See p. 43 for suggestions.

PROPAGATION TIPS

Seeds
Good time for sowing houseplants and perennial herbs; one of main months for annuals: tomatoes, aubergines, peppers, chillies, herbs, ipomoea, thunbergia.

Cuttings
Could take leaf cuttings or stem cuttings of particularly easy plants; separate and pot offsets.

Bulbs
Hippeastrum, achimenes, sinningia, tuberous-rooted begonias, reichsteineria, and lilies can be started into growth.

STARTING PLANTS INTO GROWTH

Campanula isophylla is an easy flowering plant covered in white bell flowers and trailing over the edges of its pot; it flowers from July to early winter, when it should be cut right down and left to rest in a cool place. New growth will be started about now by moving the plant to a warm place and watering generously.

Hippeastrum bulbs, achimenes and begonia tubers, and sinningia (gloxinia) corms can still be started into growth if you haven't done so already (see p. 11).

AS PLANTS DIE DOWN

Cyclamen should now be dried off (if you didn't do this in February), and stored in a cool place until the time comes to bring them into growth again in the autumn. Alternatively you can discard them and buy new plants next year. If you haven't done so already cut back solanums if you want to keep them for next year (see p. 93).

WATERING AND SPRAYING

WHEN TO WATER

It is almost too well known to repeat that more plants die from over-enthusiastic watering than from any other cause. The questions people always ask are 'How much water?' and 'How often?' – questions that it is unfortunately quite impossible to answer in a dogmatic way as it all depends on the time of year, the temperature, the light, the compost the plant lives in, and the likes and dislikes of the plant itself (see Glossary). To make things even more difficult, opinions differ so much: one person's moist is another person's nearly dry. The best advice is to err always on the side of too little water rather than too much; plants can withstand slight drought far better than waterlogging, so give less than you think. Plants must be kept moderately moist, never soggy, and should never stand in a saucer of water that has drained through the compost (though there are exceptions, like the beautiful cyperus from the banks of the Nile, which *must* stand in water to be really happy). As long as you keep an eye on them plants usually survive; fortunately they are amazingly tolerant. For the real worriers there are moisture meters available.

Plants in clay pots need more watering than those in plastic pots as water is lost through the porous clay, and those in a loam-based compost (John Innes type) need more than those in a peaty compost, as peat mixtures tend to keep moist for longer. Plants on a sunny window sill need more than those in a shady corner; plants outside, particularly in summer, need a lot. Give more water when plants are obviously growing fast and less when they are dormant; resting plants in a centrally heated room will need more than similar plants in a cooler place.

All the above perhaps demonstrates how difficult it is to be dogmatic about watering.

HOW TO WATER

Look at your plants every day. If the surface of the soil looks dry then it needs water; it seems better to let a plant get nearly dry (though never quite) and then give a lot of water, than to give daily drips and drops. This is particularly true of cacti and succulents, and, though to a lesser extent, evergreens with thick, fleshy leaves; all these can bear periods of dryness, so their compost should be allowed to become almost dry before watering again.

Sometimes a plant becomes so dry that the soil ball (the soil in the pot containing the roots) shrinks, and gaps appear round the edges of the pot so that the water runs straight through; the pot must be immersed in a bowl, sink or bucket of water when this happens, with water three-quarters of the way up the sides, and left there until bubbles stop rising to the surface and the top of the compost is damp. A wilting plant usually stages a dramatic recovery when given this treatment.

For most plants water poured gently from a narrow-spouted watering can is best. For plants that need generous amounts of water the pot should be filled to the brim, and any water which drains from the pot into the saucer must be poured away. Plants in need of refreshing can be stood in a sink and watered with a can with a fine rose, giving them a shower bath. Even better than this is a real shower bath in light rain outside if this can be managed. There is nothing like rain water for plants if you live in a hard water area. Those lucky enough to live in a soft water area may not have such strong teeth but their finger nails and indoor plants will be extremely healthy.

Small pots can be watered by standing them in a bucket, bowl or sink, and for peaty compost which has become dry this is the best way (see above).

Self-watering pots

FOOD PLANTS

In March I like to sow green peppers and chillies (though you can sow them in February, see p. 18). These do well in a warm, bright place, and should produce fruit. The chillies look good for a long time; then you can cut them and dry them and hang them up on a wall in winter to furnish you with hot little dried fruits for curries, as well as looking very decorative. You can also sow tomatoes if you haven't already done so. (See p. 19 for general tips on sowing seed.)

Round about the middle of the month the small tomato seedlings will be ready to be potted up (if you sowed seed in February). I like to do this in 5–8 cm (2–3 in) pots so that they can make good little plants before the final planting into gro-bags or large containers in a month's time.

HERBS

Parsley is a herb I must have and that too gets sown now, together with basil, summer savory, chervil, dill and pot marjoram. You could also sow any of the perennial herbs. All these look good in kitchens, smell gorgeous, and also keep the flies away. In Greece young girls used to stand a pot of basil in the window as a sign that it was safe for their lover to call. As the pots also stand about to keep flies away this must have caused a certain amount of confusion at times. (See p. 46 for tips on sowing seed.)

FLOWERING PLANTS

The second week of March is the time when some of my very favourite seeds go in, those of ipomoea, morning glory – *I. rubro-caerulea* (syn. *I. tricolor*) 'Heavenly

SELF-WATERING POTS

There are a number of pots or jardinières, to use an old term (nowadays they are called planters – not a lovely word in my opinion but never mind), which take a lot of the worry out of watering. These are pots or troughs – sometimes in innocuous plastic, sometimes with a brass or copper finish – with a water reservoir, from which the water is taken up into the pots by wicks, thus automatically keeping the compost at the right level of moisture. They can vary in size from individual pots to large troughs on castors which hold a group of plants, and the reservoirs must be filled every 3 or 4 weeks.

Some of these are for plants in compost-filled pots, some are for use in hydroponic growing (see p. 72). They are ideal for people who have a great deal to do and don't want to be bothered with normal watering, or for those who are away a lot of the time. They work best for plants which like to be permanently moist. Names to look out for among others are Hawes Elliots, Geeco Products, Grosfillex, Vastill, and EMSA. There are also hanging and wall pots with saucers which can be filled with grit to act as reservoirs and reduce watering to a minimum.

There is also an automatic watering system available which has a central reservoir of water from which protrude a number of glass-fibre wicks which are inserted into the pots; a similar version could be made at home with a jug or pot with thick string, plaited wool, or glass-fibre wicks.

SPRAYING

Plants do not only take in water through their roots; a great deal is absorbed by the foliage, too, so it is important to spray the leaves to keep them free of dust, which would clog the pores. Spraying also helps provide the humidity many plants need. Damp-lovers like ferns need a very humid atmosphere and will benefit from a lot of spraying. In fact all plants, except cacti and succulents, and the hairy or furry-leaved characters, love a mist-spray every day or so, particularly in dry or centrally heated conditions.

FEEDING

WHEN TO FEED

Around March you not only start to give more water to the plants, you also start to feed them. In their natural habitats the correct chemical nutrients are found in the soil or they would not be growing there in the first place. So certain plants grow better in some places than in others. In the natural world outside the windows the soil is constantly replenished by dying vegetation and falling leaves. This humus keeps the soil soft, crumbly and porous, able to hold both moisture and air; it also makes it more acid, thus enabling the roots to absorb the nutrients the plant needs. Plants indoors and out need to be fed to keep healthy.

A plant potted in fresh compost of the right mixture will live for 6 months on the nutrients in the mixture and the same is true of plants you have just bought. As the months go by the plant will use them up. The faster it grows the more quickly they are consumed, so a quick-growing plant in good condition must be given more food than a slow grower. In almost all cases the winter is the dormant or resting time for plants, particularly if they are in a cool situation. When the growth rate slows down at the end of the summer feeding should be stopped, and not started again until the spring. Growth should be very noticeably going on when you start feeding. Plants need fertilizer when they are in full flood as regards leaf and bud, and not when resting, in full flower, or seedlings.

HOW TO FEED

The easiest way to feed a plant is with a liquid fertilizer, as these are given at the time of watering. Never put plant food into a dry compost, it must be moist.

Never give more fertilizer than is recommended on the label, thinking that you, or the poor plant, cannot have too much of a good thing. You, or rather it, can. Six drops means just that and no more, and once a fortnight means that too, although it will do no harm to give half the amount twice as often.

Some plant foods are applied in drops, some come as powders which you mix with water, some are granular, which you sprinkle over the compost, and some come in the form of tablets or sticks which are pushed into the compost and release the food over a period. Take your pick. I like the plastic dropper with a seaweed food, but there are plenty to choose from. One of the latest is a capillary mat which sits in the saucer retaining moisture and releasing fertilizer slowly up into the pot.

Once you have started feeding plants then you should continue throughout the growing season. Most plants which have not been repotted in the last 6 months, or last summer, will need feeding, as the compost will have lost its 'goodness'. Plants which have come through the winter happily and are waking up will need feeding every week or two from March or April to August or September.

You can usually see that a plant needs food if it is growing slowly or not at all, and is generally lacking strength and vigour. Not only houseplants need feeding – if you have annual flowers or vegetables or herbs they should be given food too, in the case of flowers when the buds start showing.

What do these plant foods contain? Nitrogen for green healthy leaves, phosphorus for strong stems and roots, and potassium for good growth and flowering or fruiting, plus trace elements such as are found in natural soil.

Blue'. There are always some plants one would not like to be without, and this is one of mine. I was getting twenty brilliant blue flowers every day last July, and as the plants were in a glazed porch and had the height available they were climbing and cascading about 3 m (10 ft) up. They will also do well climbing up strings or bamboo poles in a sunny window, and there is no blue flower to touch them for colour. I usually put three or four seeds in a 15 cm (6 in) pot or five or six in a 25 cm (10 in) pot, and pot them on when their true leaves show, four or five to a 30 cm (12 in) pot, but you could perfectly well just leave them in the original pots.

Another annual climber you might try is thunbergia, black-eyed Susan. Like ipomoea, this does well either inside or out. I would always sow seed inside and plant outside later when all danger of frost is passed. (See opposite for more about flowering annuals, and p. 19 for more on sowing seed.)

TOP-DRESSING

If you have a window box or large container outside this is a good time to remove the top few centimetres of compost and replace it with fresh before planting.

FLOWERING ANNUALS

BEDDING PLANTS AS HOUSEPLANTS

There are always lots of flowering annuals on sale as bedding plants at garden shops and greengrocers in May, and many make very good temporary houseplants, as well as giving you a whole summer of colour in a window box. Petunias, heliotrope (although it can be kept through the winter it is usually treated as an annual), African and French marigolds, mignonette and verbena will all flower right through the summer indoors or out. Godetias (the small varieties), pansies, dwarf antirrhinums (snapdragon) and the silver-leaved senecio are also good value for window boxes and other containers outside.

There is something particularly exciting about seeing the little plants being put in their boxes in May ready to get going in their speedy annual way. Sweet williams, wallflowers and forget-me-nots can be put in in the autumn to flower next spring or early summer.

As with herbs and food plants, all these can be grown from seed, but you will end up with more than you need, and it is generally better to buy them as small plants.

GROWING PLANTS FROM SEED

There are some flowering annuals, however, that one never sees as plants – among these one of my absolute favourites, ipomoea, morning glory. The brilliant blue trumpet flowers of *Ipomoea rubro-caerulea* (syn. *I. tricolor*) 'Heavenly Blue' last only one day, but if you keep watering, feeding and dead-heading it will produce more each day. Growing up to 2 m (7 ft) or more, it can make a curtain of flowers at a window. Sow seed in March or April (peat or loam compost will do), find the brightest, sunniest position possible, keep the compost just moist, spray occasionally, particularly when it is flowering, and give a feed once a fortnight from about June onwards, and you should have these wonderful flowers from July to October.

Another good annual to grow from seed is thunbergia, black-eyed Susan. The variety used as an annual pot plant indoors or out is *T. alata*; it has yellow or white flowers with a dark centre, and will grow up canes or wires to 3 m (10 ft) in a season. Treat as ipomoea, except that you should add a little lime to the compost before planting, and once again you should have flowers from July to October.

You can also grow nasturtiums from seed. Just push the seeds a few centimetres into the soil in May and they will be trailing all over the place by the end of the summer, providing masses of greenery and splashes of vivid red and orange.

The important thing to remember about all flowering annuals, whether you buy them as little plants or grow them from seed, is that they have a lot of growing to do in the one year so they will need a lot of water and regular feeding. And dead flowers must be rigorously removed to make them last as long as possible.

Ipomoea

Thunbergia alata

Plants to Buy

FOR THE HOUSE

There is a certain amount of extra plant buying this month, for Mothering Sunday. Very often little bowls of mixed plants are given as gifts; these do very well for a time but soon the plants must be separated and potted up singly or the larger and stronger growers will swamp the smaller and weaker ones.

Clivia miniata is a plant worth looking out for. It is an undemanding plant, and will be flowering now, with huge orange heads of flowers. And you should still be able to find hippeastrum bulbs, achimenes and begonia tubers, and sinningia (gloxinia) corms.

If you are buying plants you will still need to be careful that they don't get too cold on the way home, as March can still produce some very cold weather.

FOR OUTSIDE

While the last hyacinths and daffodils will still be brightening your rooms, the best window boxes now are often mixtures of dwarf conifers and daffodils. Incidentally, this is a good time to order these dwarf conifers. There are many small cypresses, as well as the little junipers and spruces (picea).

Another plant that goes well with the dwarf conifers is heather. Heathers are amazingly tough little plants, often flowering in the snow. This is a good time to plant them in window boxes and other containers outside, to flower in the late summer, autumn and winter. Some are available by post from the nurseries. See p. 85 for suggestions as to dwarf conifers and heathers that are suitable for window boxes.

If you haven't yet done so, you would still just have time to order plants for putting out in window boxes or pots outside such as begonias and geraniums, but wait until May, when there is no likelihood of frost, before planting outside.

Think, too, about what you are likely to need in the coming months in the way of bags of compost, plant food, sand, grit, special compost mixtures, canes, twine, seed trays, etc., both for the annuals and for the houseplants proper.

APRIL

If the first suggestions of spring came in March, in April spring is truly with us. This is in all ways the best of months, with the apple blossom, the flowering cherries, the primroses and the violets. The busy bees make their appearance and the evenings get longer. Easter usually comes this month, always Shakespeare's birthday, April Fools' Day, and the opening of the cricket season. April brings the sweet spring showers, which bring in their turn the flowers that bloom in May. As the sun grows hotter, the days may be warm and moist, but there is still sometimes frost at night, and occasionally even snow, though never for long.

April is one of the busiest months in the garden, and even with plants in the house there is plenty to do. This is the main month for repotting and potting on, and a good month for taking cuttings. You could still be sowing annual seeds, but in any case your seedlings will need potting and careful watering. All the houseplants will be in strong growth by now, needing ever more water and regular feeding. The window boxes should be cleared, and got ready for planting out next month. The thing to remember is that everything you do now will be abundantly rewarded later in the year.

APRIL

TO BUY

A GOOD TIME TO BUY CITRUS PLANTS – INDEED MOST HOUSEPLANTS

MANY POT-GROWN PLANTS AVAILABLE FOR INDOORS AND FOR WINDOW BOXES – GERANIUMS, PELARGONIUMS, *BEGONIA SEMPERFLORENS*, LOBELIAS, FUCHSIAS, PETUNIAS, HERBS

IN FLOWER

BRUNFELSIA, PELARGONIUMS, SPATHIPHYLLUM AND STRELITZIA STARTING TO FLOWER

CLIVIA, HIPPEASTRUM, KALANCHOE, RHIPSALIDOPSIS AND ZANTEDESCHIA STILL IN FLOWER

CINERARIA, JASMINE AND PAPHIOPEDILUM FINISHING

OUTSIDE FORGET-ME-NOTS, PANSIES, POLYANTHUS, PRIMROSES AND WALLFLOWERS WILL BE FLOWERING ALONGSIDE THE LAST OF THE SPRING BULBS

1 Philodendron selloum
2 Crocus
3 Dracaena deremensis
4 Hippeastrum
5 Caladium
6 Tulipa tarda
7 Brunfelsia calycina

Looking After Your Houseplants

WATERING, FEEDING

As so much growth is going on (it is so exciting when you can actually *see* the difference from day to day), you will have to water generously, and feed weekly or fortnightly (to help you remember *when* it is a good idea to feed always at the same time and on the same day of the week).

Cacti and succulents will have been almost dry (not quite) in the winter, and slightly more water will have been given last month, or even at the end of February. This month they can have more generous amounts of water as this will help to plump them up and encourage them to flower. It is always quite a big moment when the little rebutias first sprout their buds, buds which turn into the most amazingly out-of-scale scarlet and crimson flowers.

HUMIDITY

You should be able to have the windows open much more now, which all your plants will appreciate, and on mild, dampish days you might even put them outside. Most of them would probably enjoy a bath in one of those sweet April showers – provided the rain isn't too heavy! In any case keep up the mist-spraying to make sure plants have the humidity they need (but keep your spray well away from the cacti and succulents).

POSITION

As the days get longer and warmer, you may find you have to move some plants away from the hottest, sunniest places. Geraniums, cacti and succulents are all great sunbathers, though, and need the warmest, brightest spots possible.

POTTING ON AND REPOTTING

WHAT COMPOST TO USE

Generally speaking the new compost should be the same as the old – you can easily tell as loam mixes are light in colour and heavy while peat-based mixes are dark in colour and lighter in weight. Most plants nowadays come in peat composts. Occasionally you acquire plants which are growing quite well but which might be happier in a different mixture. I bought a beautiful thorny *Euphorbia milii*, for example, in a small pot of peat compost in which the cutting had been rooted. It was healthy, but is doing much better now that I have transferred it to a pot of John Innes No. 2 (see Glossary for preferred composts).

POTTING ON

To see if a plant wants potting on turn it upside down with one hand on the surface of the soil, the fingers supporting the plant (use gloves if spiky); gently shake it or tap the pot edge on a table or bench, and the soil ball should slide out. For large pots and plants you will obviously need help. You will soon see if it needs a larger home as the roots will be thickly woven round the edge. This should ideally be done in late spring, but can be done any time in spring or summer, never later than September unless it is urgent. If you do it in hot weather make sure you keep the plant moist and shaded for a few days to give it time to re-establish itself in the new pot. Do it about 4 days after the plant has had a good watering.

If the new pot is a clay one it should be soaked in water for a day or the clay will suck all the water from the plant. Old pots must be washed well. Again, if it is clay, the new pot will need a crock (a piece of old broken flower pot) over the drainage hole. Plastic pots with their several small drainage holes do not need crocks. Put a layer of the new compost in, gently tease the roots out of the old soil, perhaps scraping gently with an old fork,

Remove the soil ball

Tease the roots out of the old soil

Place plant in new pot

Fill pot with new compost

till about a quarter of the old soil ball has been removed, and repot the plant, making sure that it is vertical, and that there is a good 1.5 cm (½ in) below the rim so that the water does not overflow. Put the new compost in firmly, but not rammed down, and finish with a professional tap on the side of the pot to level it off nicely.

The majority of plants go into plastic pots and peat-based compost nowadays. I do find, however, that certain plants prefer clay pots and loam-based mixes, cacti, succulents and geraniums, for example.

REPOTTING

Repotting means a change of pot and soil into a pot of the same size. This is usually for older and larger plants, and should be done every year or two. The procedure is the same. Changing the compost, teasing out the roots, and removing old dry roots, gives an older plant a new lease of life. New compost must be watered and kept moist, never ringing wet. If ferns, for example, look a bit sick the peat compost may be too wet, so take out the soil ball, squeeze out the water, tease out the roots, and put in fresh compost.

PROPAGATION TIPS

Seeds
Good time for sowing houseplants and perennial herbs; last really good month for sowing most annuals.

Cuttings
Good month for all cuttings, from now until August or September; separate and pot offsets.

Bulbs
Plant lilies.

Division
Divide large clumps if repotting mature plants.

KEEPING THE LEAVES CLEAN, TIDYING UP

If you have not already done so inspect all your plants, removing any dust or dead leaves, and generally giving them a good spring clean.

REPOTTING AND POTTING ON

The main important task this month is the repotting or potting on of pot-plants. This is the best time of year to do this, as growth has well and truly started and the plants will be making new roots. Most houseplants will need potting on after a year or two, sooner or later according to their natural growth rate. You will see that growth has slowed down, or that the plant has got quite obviously too big for its boots, and sometimes (horrors) the poor roots will be escaping through the drainage holes at the bottom of the pot.

Tradescantia, setcreasea, schefflera, heptapleurum, foliage begonias and sparmannia are some of the plants that should be potted on or repotted in April. Crassulas, dracaenas, cordylines and philodendrons will need this every second April. For detailed instructions as to what to do see p. 35.

Some plants might flop a little and look out of sorts after repotting, particularly if the weather is warm. If this happens keep them shaded for a few days and spray them with tepid water and they should soon perk up again.

TOP-DRESSING

If you haven't already done so, you should now replace the top 5–8 cm (2–3 in) of compost in the pots of large plants like hydrangeas, bay trees, heptapleurum and sparmannia. They will do much better if this is done.

SOWING SEEDS

Probably the best month for sowing most houseplant seeds, so it might be worth trying one or two, as houseplants are so expensive to buy. Only monstera prefers to wait until a little later in the year – May or June. See p. 43 for suggestions as to what you could try.

TAKING CUTTINGS

Any time from April until the end of the summer is a good time for taking stem cuttings: sparmannia, myrtle, geraniums and cane begonias are some of the plants that are easy to propagate in this way (see p. 70 for detailed instructions). Even if you do not want to root cuttings it will improve the parent plant to cut it down and shape it, thus avoiding untidy straggliness. The pieces of stem will root better if a humid atmosphere is created, so the pot with cuttings should be covered in a plastic bag and left in a warm place.

Sparmannia should have flowered in February or March, or even January, and must be pruned now as it is a great grower; it will turn into a small tree at the drop of a hat, and soon becomes too large for most rooms. I once had one which touched the ceiling and made the room rather dark; my present one is a cutting of a cutting of a cutting of this. Sparmannia is not found in every plant shop, but it is well worth searching for, with its large, soft, apple-green leaves and pretty flowers in spring. It is virtually indestructible too. Altogether one of my essential plants.

See p. 43 for suggestions as to what you could try.

TOOLS YOU WILL NEED

As you will see you will gradually amass a selection of pots, saucers, and bags of compost. Many people manage with the absolute minimum of tools, and if you have just a few houseplants to care for you will not need more. Any old spoon or fork can loosen the surface of the soil to aerate it, and water, which should be at room temperature, can be dispensed from any jug or bottle.

You may need larger *saucers* for the plant pots to stand on, or shallow trays filled with gravel or peat for plants that need humidity and moisture from below. You always need more saucers than you think, so it's a good idea to buy odd, pretty ones from junk shops.

Most plants, as we have seen, come in *plastic pots* nowadays, in a peat compost designed for them. Nevertheless, it may be worth having a few *clay pots* for the plants which like them best – cacti and succulents.

A *watering can* with a long spout is useful, especially for plants that are difficult to reach, in window boxes or hanging baskets. It should be plastic for lightness, and two small ones might be better than one large, as a gallon can, full, is heavy and difficult to manoeuvre, especially if pots are high up on a shelf. The fine rose at the end of the spout would be needed for watering small seedlings and window boxes, and for keeping the gravel bed of plant troughs moist. You will also need a *plastic bucket* for moistening peat, and for plunging in the plants that have dried up (though you could do this in a bowl or the sink), and for mixing grit into your compost mixture.

An absolutely essential piece of equipment is a plastic *mist-spray bottle* to keep up the humidity and give all the moisture-loving plants like ferns their daily shower of mist. A second spray bottle (don't get them mixed up) will be needed for insecticides and pesticides, although many of these can be bought in spray cans.

Most plant food comes in easily dispensed plastic bottles; if you use the pow-

A surprising number of stem cuttings root easily in a jar of water – ivy, tradescantia, impatiens, philodendron, heptapleurum and chlorophytum all obligingly root in this easy way, and it is worth trying peperomias too. Roots should begin to grow in a few weeks, and when the plant has produced a good set it is time to pot it in a small pot of compost.

AS PLANTS DIE DOWN

If you have been lucky enough to have cyclamen plants that have continued to flower until late March or even the beginning of April, they should now be either discarded or dried off and stored in a cool place until it is time to bring them into growth again in the autumn.

Annuals and Outdoor Plants

FOOD PLANTS

April is a bit on the late side for sowing most seeds, but you could still do so if you didn't get round to it in March. It is the most usual time for sowing aubergine seed, however. Even if sowing seed now, I would still do so in small pots inside.

Tomatoes and other fruiting annuals that were sown in good time can go into their large pots in their summer positions now, if they are to remain indoors, but planting outside in pots or window boxes is best left till May in case of frost.

All seedlings will need careful watering with the finest rose of the watering can. As mentioned before, they should be potted on as soon as the first true leaves show, as the younger they are the less root damage will take place.

HERBS

The main months for sowing herbs are March and April. If you sowed seed in March the first batches of seedlings should be ready for pricking out and potting on this month.

FLOWERING PLANTS

If you haven't sown ipomoea, morning glory, do so now rather than be without these wonderful blue flowers later in the year. Nor would it be too late to sow thunbergia.

As with the food plants, water seedlings with great care, and pot on as soon as the first leaves show.

Remove old, finished bulbs from hanging baskets and window boxes ready for the summer plantings next month. Some of the prettiest outdoor boxes at this time of year hold mixtures of forget-me-nots, wallflowers and red or yellow tulips.

der form you will need large *bottles* so that you are not constantly making up small quantities.

A sharp *knife* will be useful for removing offsets and taking cuttings, and perhaps a pair of *secateurs*, certainly a strong pair of *scissors*, for dead-heading, cutting string, and tidying up plants.

For a window box or large container outside you may need a small *trowel* and *hand fork*. The trowel will also be useful for filling large pots with compost.

A collection of *plastic bags with wire closures* will be useful for collecting seeds or cuttings, and for putting over rooting cuttings. You may need *seed boxes* and *pots with plastic domes* (see p. 19), and perhaps heated *propagators* for both seeds and cuttings. Dark plastic bags are useful for starting sinningias and begonias into growth. Large, clear plastic bags can be placed over plants, held up by canes, to conserve moisture and keep them from drying out if you are going to be away for a few days.

Bags of *compost* and *seed mixture* come in convenient small sizes, although the larger sizes are relatively cheaper. You will need *canes* to support tall plants, and *twine*, *string*, or *plastic ties* to anchor them to the stem. Small plant *labels* are nice to give the plants their correct botanical names, and also to note times of feeding. A small *brush* with soft bristles will remove dust from hairy or furry leaves, and a *soft cloth or cotton wool* can be used to wipe large leathery leaves with water.

There are various ways of watering plants when you are away (see p. 68), including self-watering pots, and you can also grow plants hydroponically (see p. 72) in special containers with no compost. A *room thermometer* is very useful as temperatures are important for houseplants. You can also buy *soil thermometers*, and *moisture gauges* for those in doubt about amounts of water.

Plants to Buy

FOR THE HOUSE

Ordinary houseplants are always best bought in the warmer months: they are growing well – or should be – and will not be badly affected by cold on their journey from the nursery or shop. Any time between now and the beginning of the autumn is fine for buying houseplants.

April seems to be a particularly good time for buying citrus plants. All the citrus family make good houseplants, with their neat, shiny leaves, although most of them need a greenhouse to do much in the way of fruiting. The easiest to find, and the prettiest, is *Citrus mitis*, the calamondin orange. Failing this, of course, you can always put some seeds in compost. One of the healthiest little grapefruit trees I know first started life on a compost heap in a north London garden.

All citrus plants will appreciate being out of doors in summer if this is possible, and for the rest of the year they like the brightest position you can give them. It is always a good idea to let them get accustomed to indoor conditions well before winter.

FOR OUTSIDE

It is getting a little late in the year for planting tubers and sowing seeds of annuals, but there should be plenty of pot-grown plants for sale in the shops, either for growing in pots indoors or for planting in window boxes and pots next month – petunias, pelargoniums, semperflorens begonias, fuchsias, herbs and many others. Even if you are buying plants for outside, it is better to buy now and keep the plants indoors until it is safe to plant outside next month. If you wait until May you may be disappointed and be unable to find the plants you want.

Geraniums could be given a particular mention here. There are new ones every year, many of which you will find to grow from seed or to buy as plantlets in the seedsmen's lists.

'Startel' is one of the newer ones, with amazing quilled petals and finely divided leaves.

Some more old-fashioned zonal pelargoniums to look out for are:

'Red Black Vesuvius', a miniature with bronzy black-lined leaves and vermilion flowers;

'Verona', with yellow leaves and pink flowers;

'A Happy Thought', with white leaves edged with green and scarlet flowers; and

'Maréchal MacMahon', with yellow and brown striped leaves and red flowers.

Scented leaves are an added delight:

P. tomentosum has furry grey leaves smelling of peppermint;

P. graveolens has fern-like leaves smelling of rose, and

P. crispum has small frizzy or curly leaves smelling of lemon.

MAY

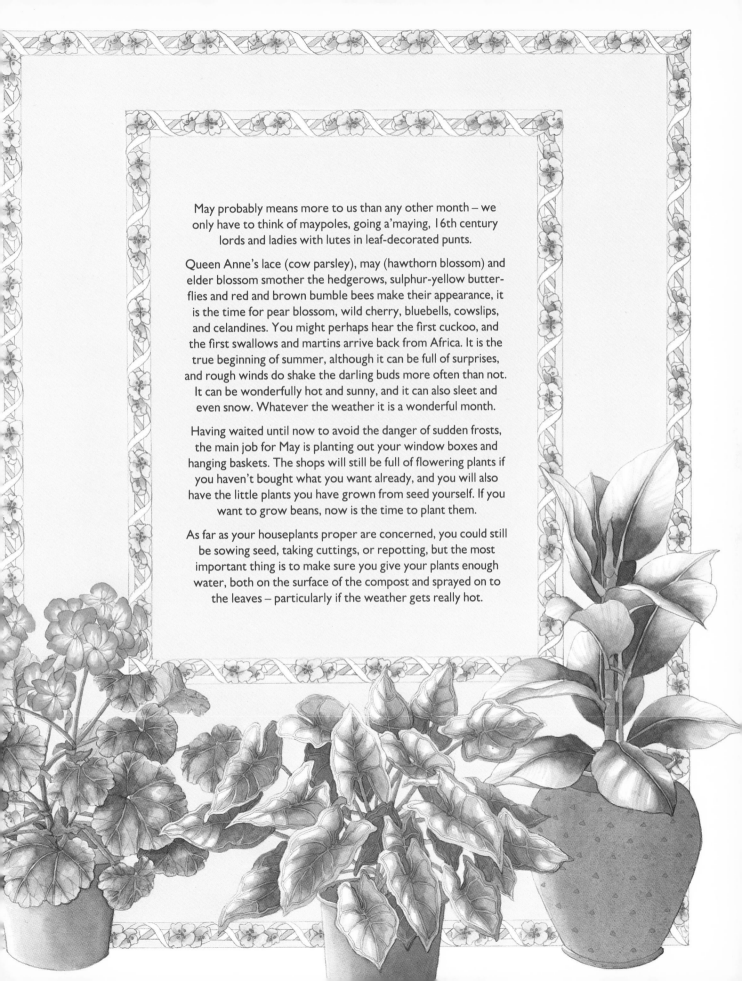

May probably means more to us than any other month – we only have to think of maypoles, going a'maying, 16th century lords and ladies with lutes in leaf-decorated punts.

Queen Anne's lace (cow parsley), may (hawthorn blossom) and elder blossom smother the hedgerows, sulphur-yellow butterflies and red and brown bumble bees make their appearance, it is the time for pear blossom, wild cherry, bluebells, cowslips, and celandines. You might perhaps hear the first cuckoo, and the first swallows and martins arrive back from Africa. It is the true beginning of summer, although it can be full of surprises, and rough winds do shake the darling buds more often than not. It can be wonderfully hot and sunny, and it can also sleet and even snow. Whatever the weather it is a wonderful month.

Having waited until now to avoid the danger of sudden frosts, the main job for May is planting out your window boxes and hanging baskets. The shops will still be full of flowering plants if you haven't bought what you want already, and you will also have the little plants you have grown from seed yourself. If you want to grow beans, now is the time to plant them.

As far as your houseplants proper are concerned, you could still be sowing seed, taking cuttings, or repotting, but the most important thing is to make sure you give your plants enough water, both on the surface of the compost and sprayed on to the leaves – particularly if the weather gets really hot.

MAY

TO BUY

FLOWERING PLANTS FOR WINDOW BOXES AND INDOORS – GERANIUMS, PELARGONIUMS, *BEGONIA SEMPERFLORENS*, LOBELIAS, FUCHSIAS, AND OTHERS

SMALL HERB PLANTS

A GOOD TIME TO BUY AFRICAN VIOLETS, DRACAENAS, AND MOST OTHER HOUSEPLANTS

IN FLOWER

MANY PLANTS STARTING TO FLOWER NOW: ABUTILON, CANE-STEMMED BEGONIAS, BELOPERONE, CROSSANDRA, FUCHSIA, HOYA, HYDRANGEA, *STEPHANOTIS FLORIBUNDA* AND STREPTOCARPUS

PLANTS THAT STARTED FLOWERING IN APRIL WILL BE IN FULL BLOOM NOW, PARTICULARLY PELARGONIUMS

HIPPEASTRUM, KALANCHOE, RHIPSALIDOPSIS AND STRELITZIA WILL BE FINISHING

OUTSIDE GERANIUMS, PETUNIAS AND SWEET WILLIAMS WILL BE STARTING

1 Heptapleurum arboricola
2 Hydrangea macrophylla
3 Streptocarpus
4 Hoya carnosa
5 Pelargonium hortorum
6 Syngonium
7 Ficus elastica

Looking After Your Houseplants

WATERING

As well as getting longer the days pack in more hours of sun now, so your plants will be needing a lot more water. As we have said before, the water for the plants must always be soft (rain water if you live in a hard water area) and at room temperature.

FEEDING

If you have not already started summer feeding of palms, dracaenas and arums, do so now, as new leaves will be forming. You should be feeding all your plants regularly by now, but these do need it more than most.

HUMIDITY

As the days get hotter your plants will need more spraying. This is if anything even more important than giving them extra water on the surface of the compost. All the plants will benefit enormously from fresh air at open windows (though not draughts), and when the weather is mild and damp they like nothing better than a shower bath outside, to freshen them up and get their leaves clean.

POSITION

Some plants, like palms, dracaenas, and arums, will have been quite happy in a south or south-west facing window in the winter and spring (though they do not need this as long as they are in a good light), but will do better if they can be moved to a cooler north or east site now that summer is a'cumin in.

SOME HOUSEPLANTS YOU CAN GROW FROM SEED

Coleus is a good, simple one to start with; February is the ideal time for sowing these and many other houseplant seeds. Sow them in seed compost or in Jiffy pots. If in trays of compost, barely cover the seeds with sifted soil, and water by standing the tray in water reaching 2 cm (¾ in) up the sides, and leaving till the surface of the soil looks moist. These can then be given the propagator treatment by placing over them inverted plastic bags held up by canes. Coleus seeds need 16–18°C (61–64°F) and germination takes 2–3 weeks. When they are large enough to handle seedlings should be potted up singly, and their tops pinched out when they are 13–15 cm (5–6 in) tall to encourage bushiness.

Coffea arabica (coffee tree) Sow in spring and summer about 1.5 cm (½ in) deep at 30°C (86°F); germination will take up to 4 or 5 weeks and plants will need a 13–15 cm (5–6 in) pot.

Musa (banana palm) is one of the largest and most splendid plants for the house. Sow the large seeds in individual small pots during spring at 18–21°C (64–70°F); germination should take 3–4 weeks. When potted on the plants grow quickly, up to 1 m (3 ft) in the first 6–12 months. Mature plants need a 25 cm (10 in) pot; repotted every year, they can reach as much as 2 m (7 ft) in 3 years, so not for the smaller rooms.

Monstera deliciosa is one of the most popular houseplants; it can be raised from ordinary seed, or from chitted (already shooting) seeds. These are sent out in May and June, which is an ideal time for sowing. Plant seeds 1.5 cm (½ in) deep in seed compost, peat or loam, with a little extra peat, and keep moist at 18–21°C (64–70°F), and they should germinate in 23–28 days. Plants will finally need 15–20 cm (6–8 in) pots.

Philodendron bipinnatifidum grows to 1–2 m (3–7 ft). It is an easy plant, and does not mind a shady place. Sow seeds on the surface of moist compost in spring and cover with plastic or glass. Germination will take place in 14–28 days at 18–24°C (64–75°F). Plant finally in a 15 cm (6 in) pot.

Fatsia japonica is a very easy houseplant with shiny, leathery leaves, growing to 1 m (3 ft). Germinates in 14–28 days at 18–24°C (64–75°F).

Grevillea robusta (silky oak) is an elegant plant with silky, fernlike leaves. Put five or six seeds in a pot; it grows up to 1 m (3 ft) and more. Germinates in 14–28 days at 18–24°C (64–75°F).

Schefflera is a long-lived and easy houseplant with umbrella-like leaves. Seed sown in spring should germinate in 21–38 days at 18–24°C (64–75°F); 21°C (70°F) is probably ideal. Pot finally in a 13–15 cm (5–6 in) pot.

These are just some of the houseplants available as seeds. Look in the seedsmen's lists for more.

SOWING SEEDS

You could still sow the seeds of some houseplants (see above), and it would be an ideal time for monstera.

Annuals and Outdoor Plants

FOOD PLANTS

Tomatoes, capsicums (sweet peppers), aubergines and chillies can all be planted outside now, in window boxes, pots or gro-bags, provided the position is sunny and sheltered. Make sure the compost is always damp, particularly just after planting. Remember that these fruiting plants will need regular feeding and plenty of water. Spraying the flowers will help them to set fruit.

Given enough depth of soil – and it should not be less than 23 cm (9 in) – climbing beans will grow quickly up strings to give you a cool, temporary curtain, sweet-smelling flowers, and some beans to eat. Unless you have a deep box and a high window it is better to choose the climbing French beans rather than the scarlet runner. They produce 'mange tout' type beans, the purple-podded varieties being particularly decorative. Seeds are sown from the end of April

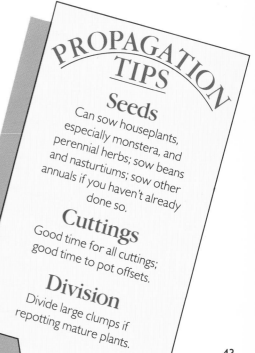

PROPAGATION TIPS

Seeds
Can sow houseplants, especially monstera, and perennial herbs; sow beans and nasturtiums; sow other annuals if you haven't already done so.

Cuttings
Good time for all cuttings; good time to pot offsets.

Division
Divide large clumps if repotting mature plants.

until June. They can be sown outside direct into window boxes or pots or they can be sown in the house in small pots and put out when a few centimetres high.

The climbing bean was after all originally grown for its decorative value alone when it reached Europe in the 17th century, and it remained a summer screening plant for 100 years before people began to take its pods seriously as a food. We get the inspiration for planting them from no less a person than Charles Dickens. In *Martin Chuzzlewit* he writes: 'His [Mr Mould's] moist glance wandered like a sunbeam through a rural screen of scarlet runners, trained on strings before the window . . .

HERBS

If you have small herb plants grown from seed they can go into window boxes now, or they can grow in pots in the house as long as they get sun, plenty of water, and fresh air. 10–13 cm (4–5 in) pots will be large enough for most of them, and ordinary potting compost will suit them.

If you have not sown seeds of annual herbs early May is just in time; there should also be plenty of plants about in the shops now, and perennials like chives, thyme and winter savory can be sown until August. Rosemary, sage, thyme and winter savory will grow easily from stem cuttings all through the summer.

FLOWERING PLANTS

Now is the time for window boxes to be planted for the summer show. The best plants are the traditional ones – geraniums, petunias, lobelias, marigolds, begonias, and fuchsias. These can be planted in a box of compost, or set in it in individual pots (see right). They may need water twice a day during hot spells. It is most important to make sure window boxes and hanging baskets are kept damp, particularly soon after planting. And don't forget to feed and dead-head regularly.

WINDOW BOXES

WINDOW BOXES

Window boxes are traditionally made of wood, painted or treated with preservative, but they can also be found in terracotta or, lighter than these, in plastic or fibreglass. About 23 cm (9 in) is the minimum depth for a box, and it should have drainage holes in the base, and be raised up from the sill on tiles or slats of wood to allow air to circulate around it. The most important thing to remember is that a box full of soil is extremely heavy, so any window box must be very securely attached to the wall, particularly if it is above the ground floor.

HOW TO USE THEM

The box can be used in two ways. Either the whole box can be filled with compost over a layer of crocks or gravel, and the plants are then put into this as into a big flower pot, or pots of plants can be put into the box, and packed round with damp peat to help keep them moist. This second way gives more scope for changing your pots of plants from time to time. Whichever method you choose the compost in the box must always be kept moist and not allowed to dry out. The compost mix in a window box need not be changed every year. As with large pots and containers the top third will need to be removed and replaced every spring before planting.

WHAT TO PLANT

In the autumn plant your window boxes with spring bulbs, heathers, dwarf conifers, forget-me-nots, wallflowers, primroses, polyanthus and sweet williams. In May plant with flowering plants such as geraniums, petunias, lobelias, African marigolds, begonias and fuchsias, with food plants such as tomatoes, peppers, aubergines and chillies, with herbs, or with plants such as climbing French beans, ipomoea (morning glory) or thunbergia, which will climb up strings to form sweet-smelling, leafy screens.

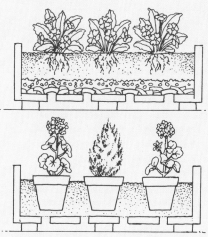

Two methods of using a window box

Don't forget that plants in window boxes will need weekly feeding while budding and fruiting, especially tomatoes, and that all plants will need frequent watering throughout the summer, twice a day if it is really hot.

HANGING BASKETS

Baskets should be at least 20 cm (8 in) in diameter, ideally 30–45 cm (12–18 in), and have a depth of 15–23 cm (6–9 in). They were traditionally lined with moss; this looks pretty, but is not that easy to obtain, so they are now lined with plastic sheeting. This plastic must have drainage holes, and holes in the side into which the roots of trailing plants can be inserted. Any good peat-based compost can be used, and it must be kept moist all the time, which again means watering twice a day in very warm summer weather. It is a good idea to take the whole basket down from time to time and immerse it in a large bowl of water to get it thoroughly soaked. Indoor hanging pots dry out quickly with heat rising, not to mention fumes, so they will need constant vigilance to see that they do not become parched.

WHERE TO PUT THEM

Hanging baskets are useful where space is short: the old canal barges and river steamers all had them; they can brighten up the dullest porch or entry, and they give a fête-like air to balconies and verandahs. They are not the easiest things in the world to site, however, as they must not entail a minor mountaineering feat every time they have to be watered, nor must they constitute a hazard for unwary heads; they also drip. Be sure to hang them from a strong support as a damp, peat-lined basket is extremely heavy. Hanging baskets outside have a hard time of it, with dry heat one day and gales the next, so try to find a place out of the prevailing wind.

WHAT TO PLANT

Outdoor hanging baskets should be planted with trailing plants such as ivies, lobelias, pendant begonias, geraniums, especially the ivy-leaved trailers, petunias and fuchsias. Chlorophytum and maidenhair ferns can be used in shady places.

For indoor hanging baskets, which are usually plastic pots with a built-in drip tray, cissus, columnea, ivies, ferns and little *Ficus pumila* are good choices; chlorophytum and tradescantia are also ideal. All these will need a certain amount of judicious pruning and shaping.

Ipomoeas, the brilliant blue 'Heavenly Blue' morning glory, will make a screen, climbing up strings either outside or inside a sunny window, as will thunbergia. If you have grown plants from seed, now is the time to plant them outside – ipomoea is one plant I could never be without. Dead-heading and mist-spraying will encourage new flowers to keep appearing.

This is also the time of year to plant and hang hanging baskets. Natural trailers are the automatic choice for these. The traditional ones are ivies, lobelias, both light and dark blue, pendant begonias, geraniums of all sorts, particularly the pretty ivy-leaved trailers, petunias, and trailing fuchsias. You can buy collections of fuchsias and geraniums by post; they will flower from June to October. Chlorophytum (spider plant) and maidenhair ferns are also good for shady places. Nasturtium seeds can be pushed in among the plants to add their vermilion and yellow flowers and tendrils at the end of the summer.

Plants to Buy

FOR WINDOW BOXES AND OTHER CONTAINERS

The choice of flowering plants for boxes and pots will be enormous around now. It is always very cheering to see boxes of lobelia and small geraniums outside the greengrocer's, although to be absolutely safe from sudden frosts it is best to postpone planting outside until the second half of the month, and until June in the north. Good little plants, both in window boxes and pots, which start flowering in March and last right through to the autumn, are semperflorens begonias – and semperflorens (always flowering) is right. Their flowers are white or pink and the small leaves often bronzy. They can be planted outside in May.

Although I have a collection of old favourite geraniums I always seem to acquire more, either as bought plants or as snippets from friends which I root. Some of the scented-leaved ones make good plants in a sunny window, and pruning keeps them tidy; their flowers are for the most part unexciting, small and pink, but the leaves are delicious and smell of rose or lemon when touched. One of the smells of summer to me.

Fuchsia plants are also available now. They can be put on the kitchen window sill or any other sunny place, or planted outside in boxes or hanging baskets.

There will also be plenty of small herb plants in the shops now. These can go on a sunny window sill or outside in a window box.

SAINTPAULIAS AND DRACAENAS

Like April, this is a good time of year to buy most houseplants, including saintpaulias (African violets). These are not among my favourite plants, and as a result I have never been successful with them. But many people are, and no book on houseplants would be complete without a mention of them. The foremost grower says: never water them until the plants start to wilt, sometimes only once every 2–3 weeks, then soak the pots in 2–3 cm (1 in) of water for 2 hours then drain them. He says the ideal temperature is 24°C (75°F), in a humid conservatory, but 18°C (64°F) is better for a room, though growth will be slower. A north window in summer, a south one in winter with nights in a warm room, and a feed once a month, should keep them happy. (Stop feeding from November to February to give them a rest.) One day, when I have time, I will try again, as the differences in the size and shape of these little flowers are amazing. Like many plants they seem to enjoy company and do best in groups.

If you are buying dracaenas don't be surprised if they lose some of their lower leaves when they come from the nursery or shop. This is a result of the change to somewhat drier conditions, but there is no need to worry about this as they soon settle in, particularly if regularly sprayed with soft water.

HOUSEPLANTS WITH COLOURFUL FOLIAGE

COLEUS

For vividly coloured leaves the old favourite coleus, the flame nettle, takes a lot of beating. These are sold everywhere in amazing colour combinations of yellow, jade-green, crimson and bronze; they make good pot plants, both indoors and outside in boxes. They are the easiest of plants to grow from seed from February to April (see p. 43). The seedlings should be pricked off early and potted into individual pots when 5–8 cm (2–3 in) high, and the central growing point of the plant pinched out when 13–15 cm (5–6 in) high to encourage a bushy shape. The dull flowers should be removed to get the best from the astounding leaves.

IRESINE

Coleus needs to be in a sunny place for the rich colours to give of their best, and so does the lesser-known iresine. This has wine-purple leaves with red veins and stems, and is quite happy outside in summer. The plants are short-lived but new ones will grow easily from cuttings.

SETCREASEA

Setcreasea is another purple plant with a bloom on leaves and stem, a large cousin of the tradescantia. This plant grows horizontally, which is unusual, and needs to be kept tidy by having cuttings taken off it from time to time. It likes a light place in summer, and does not mind cool conditions in winter.

HERBS

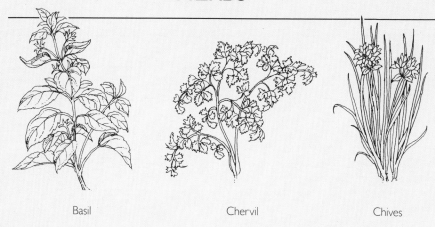

Basil   Chervil   Chives

The best herbs for the house, both for the kitchen window sill and for the window box, are the small-scale ones. You can grow fennel, for example, but it will be a small plant compared with its brother in the garden. Good herbs for the sill are pot marjoram, thyme, sage, rosemary, summer and winter savory, chives, chervil, dill, basil, and parsley. Sage, rosemary, chives, winter savory and thyme are perennial plants; all the others are annuals and have to be grown from seed or bought every year. As a rule it is best to buy plants; they are cheap and easy to find.

If you grow them from seed it is easy to sow tiny rows in a seed pan of compost, under a plastic dome. Sow a row of, say, basil, parsley, marjoram, dill and summer savory, and sage perhaps as a perennial. These are sown in March or April; when they come up and show their first true leaves they can be potted into individual pots, one plant into a 10 cm (4 in) pot or three to a 15 cm (6 in) pot. They will grow easily indoors on a sunny sill, but they need as much fresh air as possible. Alternatively they can be grown outside in a window box, either planted directly in the compost or set in the box in their pots and packed round with peat or peat compost.

Perennial herbs will survive the winter in a cool place and should start leafing again in the spring, but will do better outside. Rosemary is a large perennial and will eventually need a big pot; again it is

better outside but should do indoors in an airy place.

Since most herbs come from the Mediterranean regions it is important not to overwater them.

When you cut herbs to dry for winter, hang them in an airy place or spread them out to dry in the sun for a few days; rub them lightly between the palms and store in airtight jars. The best time to cut herbs for drying is just before they flower, as it is then that the essential oils are at their strongest.

Basil is to me the most precious of all the herbs – its pungent, sweet scent is quite amazing, the very meaning of summer, and it is excellent with tomatoes. It came originally from India where it is sacred to Vishnu and Krishna, and was grown in the temples. It is a herb of love in Greece and Italy and an essential window sill plant in hot countries. I always mean to have a plant in every room in the house.

Basil is a herb which really must be used fresh; the leaves can be dried and are useful in the winter, but the scent and taste are very different. Both the sweet and the bush varieties make excellent houseplants – even in the hottest summers basil usually does much better in a pot inside than out. Six basil seedlings in a 20 cm (8 in) pot with the tops pinched out will give you sweet-smelling little bushes. You can also try sowing basil in late summer which will give you supplies during the winter.

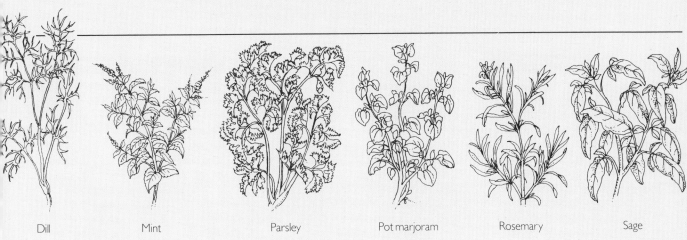

Dill   Mint   Parsley   Pot marjoram   Rosemary   Sage

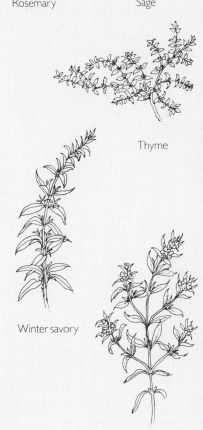

Thyme

Winter savory

Summer savory

Chervil is a pretty, aniseed-flavoured, feathery plant, a member of the parsley family; it comes from the Mediterranean and was spread by the Romans. It was used, apart from cooking (part of *les fines herbes*), as a preventative against the plague, a cure for hiccoughs, and a reliever of rheumatics and bruises. It does well in rooms as, unlike most herbs, it is happy in shade.

Chives are of the onion family and the most ancient of herbs. The Chinese used them in 3000 BC, and in the Middle Ages they were used with food, particularly eggs and fish, as well as as an antidote to pain and a remedy for bleeding. You can divide clumps if they get too large.

Dill is named after a lovely Norse word 'dilla' meaning 'to lull', as this herb has a mildly soporific effect. Dill water soothes babies and dill tea helps sleep. It comes from Asia Minor and the Egyptians used it 5,000 years ago. It was used in perfumes in Greece and Rome, and as a lucky herb for wreaths and bridal posies.

Mint is not really very suitable as a houseplant as it is a rampant grower and must be grown alone. If you do want to grow it you can put in roots from March to May if they are kept damp; a large pot or 5 litre (1 gallon) bucket will be needed.

Parsley must be the most widely used of all herbs; according to the Greeks it was the herb of Hercules and was woven into victors' crowns; it was also thought to delay drunkenness, to prevent baldness, and to be best if sown on Good

Friday, if possible by a pregnant woman.

Parsley is ideal both for window boxes and for pots inside in good light. It can be kept on the window sill right through the winter to give fresh parsley when it would be affected by frost outside.

Pot marjoram is a very old herb from the eastern Mediterranean, also spread by the Romans. It is good for meat cooking. It seems to increase in pungency and strength when dried.

Rosemary was once named Dew of the Sea. It was a strewing herb, popular with the Elizabethans, always a symbol of constancy and remembrance, and used in posies against the plague. It has always been known — apart from its use in cooking, especially with lamb — to be good for the skin and hair.

Sage was used by the Greeks to preserve memory, to remove depression, to retard the effects of old age, to cure consumption, snake bites and grief. Its many uses are demonstrated by the old saying: 'How can a man die who has sage in his garden?' Sage tea used to be a popular drink, and the Chinese were glad to try it when the traders first brought 'Tea' tea to the West.

Thyme has been popular since ancient times for its pungent flavour in cooking and its medicinal properties. It was a symbol for courage in Greece and a cure for shyness in the Middle Ages.

Winter and summer savory are cheering herbs used in cooking in the same way as thyme. They were also used in olden

times to brighten eyes, cure ear complaints, and soothe insect stings, and by the Ancient Egyptians as an aphrodisiac. Savory was popular with both Romans and Saxons, and has for long been a favourite window box or pot herb. Winter savory is a perennial, summer savory an annual.

DRACAENAS AND CORDYLINES

DRACAENAS

Dracaenas must be given a short eulogy here, as they are among the easiest plants to grow and always get admired. They must be among the most ideal plants for the house, becoming tall and tree-like as the lower leaves fall, with a fountain of stiff, narrow, lance-shaped leaves at the top. They grow straight up and produce no offsets. Although they come from the tropics and sub-tropics they are not at all fussy and are happy in a hall, living room or kitchen.

D. marginata is the toughest of the family, although it looks delicate. In fact, it is one of the strongest houseplants in the world. It has very narrow leaves, green edged with red, or, in the case of *D. m.* 'Variegata', green with creamy yellow and pink stripes like pyjamas.

D. fragrans has curving leaves in a graceful rosette and was a Victorian favourite for pedestals.

D. deremensis has striped silver and green leaves and will grow to 1.2 m (4 ft) or more.

D. sanderiana is smaller and covered in leaves.

All these are happiest in a warm room, though *D. marginata* is very tolerant. They like a lot of water in summer, and occasional spells outside during the day; in winter they need little water, and a temperature not less than 10–12°C (50–54°F). A north-west or south-east window will suit them. Repot them every second April in ordinary potting compost, adding a little peat if you use a loam-based compost. As these plants have tall stems in the fullness of time, a group of them of varying heights is very effective.

CORDYLINES

Cordylines are similar to dracaenas in looks, but they do not grow so tall and the leaves are club-shaped rather than lance-shaped. As a family they are more delicate, and really happier in a greenhouse, but the crimson-leaved varieties are hardier than the others and make good houseplants in a living room or kitchen as long as the winter temperature does not go below 12–16°C (54–61°F). Like dracaenas they should be repotted every second April and given a feed every 2 weeks in summer. The crimson leaves, with the light shining pinkly through them, are very decorative. A tougher houseplant is *C. australis*, with a fountain of long narrow leaves.

JUNE

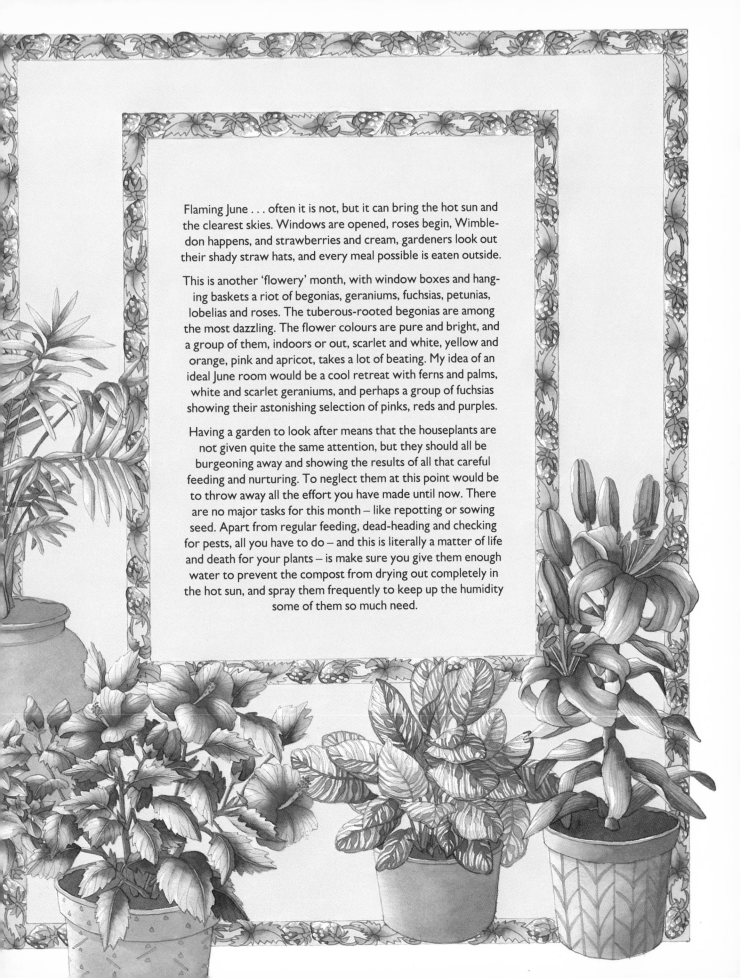

Flaming June . . . often it is not, but it can bring the hot sun and the clearest skies. Windows are opened, roses begin, Wimbledon happens, and strawberries and cream, gardeners look out their shady straw hats, and every meal possible is eaten outside.

This is another 'flowery' month, with window boxes and hanging baskets a riot of begonias, geraniums, fuchsias, petunias, lobelias and roses. The tuberous-rooted begonias are among the most dazzling. The flower colours are pure and bright, and a group of them, indoors or out, scarlet and white, yellow and orange, pink and apricot, takes a lot of beating. My idea of an ideal June room would be a cool retreat with ferns and palms, white and scarlet geraniums, and perhaps a group of fuchsias showing their astonishing selection of pinks, reds and purples.

Having a garden to look after means that the houseplants are not given quite the same attention, but they should all be burgeoning away and showing the results of all that careful feeding and nurturing. To neglect them at this point would be to throw away all the effort you have made until now. There are no major tasks for this month – like repotting or sowing seed. Apart from regular feeding, dead-heading and checking for pests, all you have to do – and this is literally a matter of life and death for your plants – is make sure you give them enough water to prevent the compost from drying out completely in the hot sun, and spray them frequently to keep up the humidity some of them so much need.

JUNE

TO BUY

A GOOD TIME TO BUY MOST HOUSEPLANTS

EXACUM AFFINE WILL BE SOLD IN FLOWER NOW, AS WILL ACHIMENES AND SINNINGIAS

BEGONIAS, PELARGONIUMS, FUCHSIAS AND OTHER SUMMER-FLOWERING PLANTS STILL AVAILABLE

IN FLOWER

ACHIMENES, TUBEROUS-ROOTED BEGONIAS, BROWALLIA, *EXACUM AFFINE*, LILIES, ROSES, SINNINGIAS AND SAXIFRAGA ALL STARTING TO FLOWER

ALL THE FLOWERS THAT STARTED IN MAY WILL NOW BE IN FULL BLOOM

ZANTEDESCHIA FINISHING

OUTSIDE HELIOTROPE, HYDRANGEAS, LOBELIA, MARIGOLDS, REGAL PELARGONIUMS, AND ROSES WILL BE COMING INTO FLOWER

1	Fuchsia
2	Pelargonium
3	Lobelia
4	Lilium hybrid
5	Pelargonium domesticum
6	Rosa chinensis
7	Exacum affine
8	Chamaedorea elegans
9	Hibiscus rosa-sinensis
10	Calathea mackoyana
11	Lilium hybrid

Looking After Your Houseplants

WATERING, FEEDING

From now until August it is almost impossible to overwater most plants, though you need to be careful with cacti as they can collapse completely if they have too much water. Don't forget the feeding, as your plants will be in full growth now, and producing flowers and fruit.

HUMIDITY

As the air tends to be dry it is vital to keep up the humidity on hot days – just as vital, in fact, as it is in artificially warm winter rooms. Ferns will need daily spraying, and all your plants will benefit from having the windows open whenever possible for maximum fresh air.

Flowering plants will last longer if they are kept moist and sprayed, and moved out of the sun at the hottest time of day – except for geraniums, which like to bask in the sun.

POSITION

The days are now the longest of the year. As the light intensifies and the sun gets hotter some of the plants inside may need moving. Cacti and succulents should be in the hottest, sunniest places possible to encourage them to flower, as should geraniums and pelargoniums, but some plants will definitely want to be away from windows and in the shade. Palms, dracaenas, arums and aspidistras are among these; palms, particularly, can become scorched and brown if they get too much summer sun. You should already have moved your plants into suitable positions for the summer, but if you haven't do so now. I usually have cyperus and ferns in the empty fireplace.

CHECKING FOR PESTS

With the roses outside and the windows open more often you must keep a weather eye out for greenfly and other aphids; they are easily abolished with a spray and must be attacked at the first glimpse.

Annuals and Outdoor Plants

FOOD PLANTS

All the annual food plants you have grown from seed – like tomatoes, capsicums (green peppers), and the highly decorative aubergines with their purple leaves and stems – should be planted outside by now, and they will need generous quantities of water and regular feeding. In fact all the plants in warm, sunny places, whether indoors or out, will need a lot of water, sometimes twice a day. Beans will fruit better if sprayed at flowering time – though the flowers of climbing beans are pretty in their own right.

BEGONIAS

Unlike pelargoniums and geraniums, which settle down almost anywhere, begonias as a species are happier in a greenhouse than in a room as they like a lot of humidity and some shade, but the Grandifloras (as you might expect – with enormous flowers up to 13 cm (5 in) across), the Pendulas (ideal for hanging baskets in a semi-shaded place, with translucent flower stems with 8 cm (3 in) flowers in a bright array of colours), and the Multifloras (with a mass of single flowers) are happy for the flowering season in a room if they are in a well-lit position, away from direct sun, and have enough water and occasional spraying (be careful no spray falls on the flowers, though, as this can mark them). In warm or hot weather the sill of an open, north-facing window would suit them well. The other main difference from geraniums is that begonias prefer plastic to clay pots, as the compost does not dry out so quickly.

TUBEROUS-ROOTED BEGONIAS
You can keep tuberous begonias (the Grandifloras, Pendulas and Multifloras) through the winter if you stop watering them when flowering finishes (around September), so that the plant dries out. You then twist the stem off the tuber when the leaves drop, and lay the pot on its side in a cool place (frostproof), or take out the tuber and store it in peat. Some time between January and April the tubers should be potted up again, hollow side up, and given very little water until growth starts up, when they have more.

FIBROUS-ROOTED BEGONIAS
The other good flowering begonias are the fibrous-rooted types like *B. semperflorens*, which can either be grown in the house, or in window boxes and tubs. The flowers are red, pink or white and the foliage green or bronzy. These little flowers go on for months if it is not too warm. 5–8 cm (2–3 in) tip cuttings can be taken at any time of year if you can be sure of a temperature of 18°C (64°F), and root easily in sand or water. They will be happy in a window box from May to September, and in the house for even longer.

CANE-STEMMED BEGONIAS
The tall cane-stemmed 'angel's wing' begonias are also of the fibrous-rooted type, and these are one of my two absolute favourites out of all the begonias. The cane-stemmed begonias have long pointed leaves, usually with reddish undersides, and flower all through the summer, with pretty pink flowers on hairy red stems. The rest of the year they make elegant foliage plants. Mine at 1.5 m (5 ft) has had to be banished to the glazed porch as there was not room for both of us in my study. They need to be sprayed fairly frequently, especially in the hot dry weather; they like semi-shade in summer, and a brighter place in winter. They also grow very easily from cuttings.

REX BEGONIAS
The rex begonias are my other favourite. These are foliage plants par excellence with their huge leaves patterned in silver, red, pink, green and near black, satiny in texture. They too need a little shade in summer and a moist environment as they come from the jungles of south-east Asia. In winter they are happy in heated living rooms as long as they are kept damp, and they seem to like artificial light. A steamy bathroom suits both these and the cane-stemmed begonias. My ancient rex, now bursting out all over with lusty leaves, was rescued from a rubbish dump as an unrecognizable stump with a withered leaf because I wanted the clay pot. It is now rewarding me for its rescue and feeding.

PROPAGATION TIPS

Seeds
Can still sow houseplants, especially monstera, and perennial herbs; last chance to sow climbing beans.

Cuttings
Good time for all cuttings; good time to separate and pot offsets.

HERBS

Pots of herbs are essential in a summer kitchen. They not only look pretty but are on hand for cooking and salads. They also help to keep flies away, and give you the benefit of their scent every time you touch them or even brush past them. All the herbs must be watered well and given fortnightly feeds, as they are fast-growing. Pinching out the flower buds will give more and larger leaves.

FLOWERING PLANTS

Apart from the houseplants proper, and the herbs and food plants, I always have to find a space for annual climbers. As I have said before, morning glory, or ipomoea, is my favourite. It will be beginning to produce its blue trumpets now, and will benefit from feeding.

My first introduction to morning glory was in the Dordogne area of France, where the little village shop was hidden by a curtain of them, and I had never seen such a blue. Equally impressive was a friend's office window sill in Soho where they made a leafy screen dotted with blue all summer long. Thunbergia is pretty, too, and I have seen summer windows adorned with climbing French beans and even cucumber vines.

Don't forget that annual plants have to pack everything into one year, and their main idea is to set seed, so they must be regularly dead-headed to give you a succession of flowers. They will also appreciate spraying on warm days.

Miniature roses, too, will benefit from mist-spraying, copious watering, and monthly feeding. They must of course be dead-headed regularly to encourage them to flower again, and they need to be watched carefully for aphids and red spider mites.

Although I have always loved succulents, with their plump leaves and extraordinary shapes, I never found spiny cacti very sympathetic until two years ago when a friend who is an avid gardener but short of space told me she was bored with her cacti and they were all going to end up on the compost heap. Did I want them? I said yes, looking rather doubtfully at the strange little prickly group I had saved from oblivion. Now, having nurtured them and fed them and sprinkled gravel round them, I find I love them dearly. They have great character. They love to sit in the summer sun, and spend the winter on a large meat dish on the spare room sill. One of the great things about cacti is that they are slow-growing, so good where space is short. A collection of a large number of different varieties can easily be accommodated on a window sill – and they do come in a bewildering variety of shapes and sizes. All this illustrates how one's feelings about plants can change. Perhaps one day I will like orchids.

THE DIFFERENCE BETWEEN CACTI AND SUCCULENTS

Both cacti and succulents are predominantly desert plants, owing their unusual and sometimes extremely bizarre appearance and shape to their need to conserve water. In many ways they are ideal as houseplants, their main needs being dry warmth in summer and dry cool in winter. The only exceptions are the 'leaf cacti', which are green and epiphytic – which means that they are air growers, growing in trees, in fissures and in angles of the branches. These grow in the forest gloom, and naturally need different treatment from the desert dwellers.

All cacti are in fact succulents – which basically means any plant which stores water – like a camel. In cacti the reserves are in the stems, and in succulents they are in the leaves – in fact cacti don't actually have any leaves. These plants are found all over the world, having adapted themselves to endure and thrive in extraordinary climates, baked by day and

MINIATURE ROSES

This is the traditional month for roses, and there are now miniature rose trees available which can be grown indoors on a sunny window sill or in window boxes and containers outside. These minute little plants begin to flower when only 5–8 cm (2–3 in) high. The flowers are red, white, pink, yellow or orange, and heights range from 10 cm (4 in) to the relative giants of 25 cm (10 in). Incredibly, most of these tiny roses actually smell sweet too. A group of them makes a delightful centrepiece on a table by a window.

HOW TO GROW THEM
These miniature roses are very easy to grow, as long as they are watered well and given a monthly feed during the growing season. Young plants are potted into 9 cm (3½ in) pots in either loam or peat-based compost. Naturally they do best in a good light: a south-west window will suit them well. They will also benefit from mist-spraying and having their pots standing on moist gravel. The ideal temperature for them is 6–10°C (43–50°F) in winter, 10–18°C (50–64°F) the rest of the year. They will need dead-heading to ensure more flowers, and any dead wood must be pruned away.

PESTS AND DISEASES
Like their large-scale relations, miniature roses must be inspected carefully for aphids in summer, and red spider mites – a spray containing pyrethrum will keep these at bay – and a quick dip in water with a little weak washing-up liquid in it will control mildew (rinse the plant off with clear water afterwards).

CACTI AND SUCCULENTS

sometimes nearly frozen at night. During dry periods succulents on the whole make little growth, packing all their growth, flowering and seeding into the rainy season. All succulents, including cacti, produce flowers, most of them brilliantly coloured, to attract insects.

The family of Cactaceae are all covered with a thick skin, and many have spines, thorns or hairs. These protect them from animal and bird predators, and also produce a little shade. There are more than 2,000 species, divided by botanists into three main tribes, Pereskieae, Opuntieae and Cereeae.

'Succulent' is a general term and does not refer to a family of plants. Succulents are all fleshy but they come from many different plant families: agaves, for instance, are cousins of the amaryllis, and gasterias of the lily.

HOW TO LOOK AFTER THEM

WATERING, FEEDING, HUMIDITY
In the summer growth period, and especially if flowering, succulents need plenty of water. As autumn comes give them gradually less; from November until March they need hardly any. Then the cycle starts up once more as they come back into the warmth and need more water again. Give them a dilute feed every 2 weeks or so in summer. They do not need humidity, so will not need to be sprayed. For the beginner with houseplants they are almost ideal, as they are undemanding and tolerant of a deal of neglect.

POSITION
All succulents need ventilation at the hottest time of year. They need plenty of light and, unlike many plants, they like to bask in hot sun in the growing season; a sunny window sill where they can get lots of air is a perfect place for them in summer. They must have a rest in winter, however, and from October to March should be somewhere where the temperature is not above 10°C (50°F) – though they are still happy in the sun, as long as it is cool.

COMPOST
All succulents need good drainage, so the soil should be open and porous. For the desert dwellers a loam-based compost is better than a peat-based one, ideally one-third of this being fine grit or coarse sand, with a sprinkling of grit or fine gravel on the surface to set off the plants. You could also use John Innes No. 1 or a special cactus mixture. The pots can be clay or plastic, though I prefer clay for these plants.

LEAF CACTI
These come from the rain forests of Central and South America, and naturally prefer a peat-based compost, again with one-third sand or grit. They need to be kept humid while budding and flowering by spraying and standing on damp pebbles or gravel. They also prefer to be out of the sun.

PESTS AND DISEASES
There is little danger of pests or disease as long as they have plenty of air and *never* too much water, so the last place to put succulents (apart from the leaf cacti) is the bathroom or kitchen where there is steam.

PROPAGATION
You can propagate cacti and succulents from seed or cuttings, but there is no doubt that cuttings or offsets are the best way for the amateur. Epiphyllums (leaf cacti) and rebutias are two which are fairly easy from seed sown in a warm place (20–25°C/68–77°F) in sandy compost, but germination may take 4 months or more.

SOME CACTI TO LOOK OUT FOR

As the cactus family is such a fascinating one, and they come in such an extraordinary collection of shapes and sizes, here are suggestions of some to look out for:

Mammillaria is the largest group or genus. These are mainly spherical, spiny balls with white hairs or spines, the flowers appearing in a little ring or crown round the top in summer.

Rebutias also come in globes, but clumps of them. Most flower when they are only a year old.

Opuntia Everybody knows the archetypal opuntia, prickly pear or rabbit's ears. Tree-sized in Western films, and used as a hedging plant round the Mediterranean, this character needs to be handled with care (and gloves) as the glochids or bristles can stick in the skin. Goethe grew this one.

Cereus is the family of the column-like or candelabra cactus, which often has a jade colour or a blue bloom.

Chamaecereus is the quick-growing peanut cactus, which consists of spiny green sausages, and will produce huge red flowers in a sunny spot.

Epiphyllums are the odd men out as they come from the steamy jungle and like humidity as well as warmth. Some flower in summer and spring, but the Christmas cactus (schlumbergera) is the opposite of most others as it flowers in the middle of the winter, and therefore has its resting and starving time in summer.

SOME SUCCULENTS TO LOOK OUT FOR

Among the succulents there are an equal number of bizarre-shaped plants. Here are some of my favourites:

Aloes Two beauties are the partridge-breasted aloe, with its patterned triangular leaves in a spiral rosette, and *A. arborescens*, the tree aloe.

Crassula argentea, the jade tree, has a stout 'trunk' and glossy plump leaves.

Gasteria makes small spiky clumps with fans and rosettes of patterned leaves; ideal for dish gardens.

Pachyphytums are the strange moon plants, with a silver-grey bloom and balloon-like leaves.

55

Plants to Buy

Although it is on the whole too late to buy annuals now, the markets and shops will still be full of brightly coloured summer-flowering pot plants, and they are a great pleasure to have in rooms. You could put their pots inside a decorative container, a pretty china bowl perhaps, or two or three in a brass pan or copper cooking pot – try white, orange and yellow begonias together. As well as begonias there are achimenes, also long-lasting and cheap to buy, the exotically coloured and spotted sinningias with their velvety trumpet-shaped flowers, and fuchsias in a bewildering variety of pinks, reds and purples. And of course geraniums and busy lizzies (impatiens), African violets, and streptocarpus, the Cape primrose.

If you are buying geraniums, do look out for the varieties with brightly patterned leaves and those with scented leaves – oak-shaped and smelling of lemon, or soft grey-green and ivy-shaped and smelling of peppermint. Scented leaves are an important part of summer.

Another very pretty houseplant that is usually on sale now is *Exacum affine*, the Persian violet. It is small, growing only to 15 cm (6 in), but it flowers until late autumn if placed in a good light, though not direct sunlight, and in a coolish temperature. The blue-mauve flowers have yellow centres and a delicious sweet scent.

And if you are thinking of buying foliage houseplants, June will be a good time, like all the other warm summer months.

JULY

Lovely July, the middle of what should be high summer and often the hottest month – although, being fickle, the climate is full of surprises, and it can be wet, particularly if anyone is organizing a fête or garden party. It should be a time for enjoying the sun, however, with the evocative murmur of honey bees on the wing and the smell of sun tan cream.

Plants that love the sun will be basking too, and bursting out with colour. Outside the hanging baskets and window boxes will be a riot of colour – geraniums, begonias, petunias, roses and a host of others all in full bloom. Inside, achimenes, sinningias, lilies and the tuberous-rooted begonias will be starting to flower, and *Campanula isophylla*, which goes on to November – a real beauty. The smells of herbs like rosemary, thyme and marjoram evoke for me the feeling of a still, hot July day, with shaded windows in cool rooms and leafy greenery in the fireplace. In fact you should now be able to start cutting and drying herbs for the winter, and your tomatoes and capsicums will be beginning to produce fruit. Your earlier efforts will thus be abundantly, and tangibly, rewarded.

As in June, the vital task for July is to keep up the watering and spraying: everything will be in full growth, and the weather can be very hot and dry. Any slacking off now and all your efforts earlier in the year could be wasted. If you go away, even for a few days, do make some arrangements for your plants. A house full of dead plants would make a poor welcome home after an enjoyable holiday

JULY

TO BUY

A GOOD MONTH TO BUY ALL HOUSEPLANTS

MANY FLOWERING PLANTS STILL AVAILABLE

ORDER BULBS FOR WINTER FLOWERING

IN FLOWER

IPOMOEA AND THUNBERGIA STARTING TO FLOWER, INSIDE AND OUT, AND NASTURTIUMS OUTSIDE

CAMPANULA ISOPHYLLA **AND HIBISCUS STARTING TO FLOWER**

MOST CACTI AND SUCCULENTS PRODUCE THEIR FLOWERS NOW OR IN AUGUST

INSIDE AND OUT ALL THE SUMMER FLOWERS ARE IN FULL GLORIOUS BLOOM

FIRST TOMATOES AND SWEET PEPPERS APPEARING

1	Yucca aloifolia
2	Dieffenbachia maculata
3	Geranium
4	Fatsia japonica
5	Howea belmoreana
6	Campanula isophylla
7	Begonia maculata

Looking After Your Houseplants

WATERING, FEEDING

As in June you must remember to give the houseplants enough water, and regular food. Hanging containers in rooms will need a lot more water in summer. If a basket or pot holds a really floppy, thirsty subject, immerse the whole thing in a bucket for 10 minutes or so, and it will revive amazingly.

Your cacti and succulents, basking on a sunny sill, may perhaps be astonishing you with their flowers. Be careful not to overwater them; globular cacti especially can collapse suddenly and soggily if too wet. And be sure they are out of the way of your mist-spray. They can be kept dust-free with a soft paint brush. These look good in dish gardens (see p. 62), with fine silver gravel spread over the top of the compost to make their own, private desert. Mentioning them makes me think again (as I often do with my plants) that it is the marvellous contrast, even with a few plants, that is such a pleasure – the large-scale leaves of palms and arums, the lacy fronds of ferns, the scarlet of the geraniums, and these stolid, plump little characters.

If you are going to be away on holiday you must make plans to ensure the plants are watered (see p. 68). If away for a few days put the plants into a shady, cool place like the bath.

HUMIDITY

In the warm, dry (hopefully) days of summer, as I keep on stressing, it is vitally important to keep up the humidity round plants, particularly ferns and arums. Spray your plants often, but take care not to splash the leaves, as this can lead to sun scorching. When spraying use the setting

FERNS

I was once in Corfu in July and August (a great mistake!) and it was so hot that all I could think about were cool grottoes with pools and ferns . . . so this month of high summer seems a good time to talk about them.

There are an enormous number of fern species, about 10,000; most of them are tropical, but we have a number in Europe which are happy in the wild woods and on walls and in gardens. As indoor plants they became very popular in the Victorian era, that great period for plant collection; they were considered so important in smart interiors that pieces of furniture were specially designed to show them off, and the Wardian case or glass plant box appeared in many elaborate shapes and varied sizes. As ferns are happy in poorly lit situations and coolish temperatures they did well, but as the years went by and central heating and large windows took the place of the Victorian twilight, ferns declined in popularity and many of the vast number then available disappeared; there are signs now that they are on the verge of a popular comeback.

Ferns, like the horsetails, those virulent and elegant weeds, belong to a plant group called the Pteridophyta, and are among the most ancient plants in the world. They existed in the Devonian period, 400 million years ago, when coal was first being formed, and have continued, much the same and without evolving, ever since. They therefore occupy a unique place in the plant world.

HOW TO KEEP THEM

As a group they are not the easiest of houseplants. Some ferns are only happy (away from their natural habitat) in enclosed plant cases or a warm greenhouse, but many are quite content in moderately cool rooms, as they like cool, moist, undisturbed places. A glass porch or bay window facing north suits them; my mother had a fernery in a porch and they are the first plants I remember.

Ferns are good on their own or in groups, as they come in such a variety of shapes and sizes, lacy or shiny, and make a happy contrast with other plants.

WATER, HUMIDITY

Most ferns that are happy in a cool greenhouse can be kept in living rooms provided they are given enough moisture and humidity. This can be supplied by placing the pots on trays of damp pebbles or in pots of damp peat and spraying the plants with a fine mist-spray daily. Even if they are watered enough they still need this extra-moist, humid environment; without it all but the most amenable turn brown and die back.

WINTER TEMPERATURES

It is dryness that is death to most ferns, and this is why many books recommend very low temperatures in winter. In a lower temperature they can also have a rest, though this is not essential to their health. However, those which come from the tropics need warmer temperatures than the hardy ferns that grow in the woods and gardens of Europe, and with this warmth they must have humidity. If this heat and humidity cannot be arranged then they will quite happily stop growing for a time in a cooler place. Ferns that need a high level of humidity will do best if you spray them frequently with the gentlest, finest mist, and stand their pots on damp pebbles or in moist peat. So make sure you give your ferns adequate humidity if you have them in an averagely warm winter room.

The winter minimum for most ferns, when they will just rest, is 12°C (54°F). The *ideal* temperature for most is 16°C (61°F). Temperatures for the individual ferns mentioned are given in the glossary.

PROPAGATION

Although packets of fern spores are sold, germination is not easy in the home; many ferns such as adiantum are easily propagated by root division, however. They are asexual or 'neuter' plants, having no flowers or seeds but powdery spores in capsules on the underside of the fronds. When these spores, which are like pollen grains, germinate they produce small triangular growths called prothalli which have both male and female organs and in their turn produce a small fern.

WHERE TO PUT THEM

The smaller ferns do well in glass cases or bottle gardens and under glass domes; *Pellaea rotundifolia* and *Adiantum capillus-veneris* are two. The large, lacy-fronded ferns like *Nephrolepsis exaltata* and *Davallia bullata* look good trailing down from a height, in a hanging container or at the top of a pillar. Two which can tolerate a warm room and a modicum of sunlight are *Asplenium nidus*, the bird's nest fern, and *Pteris cretica*, the Cretan brake.

PROPAGATION TIPS

Seeds
Can still sow houseplants and perennial herbs; sow parsley and basil for autumn supplies.

Cuttings
Good time for all cuttings; good time to pot offsets.

for the finest mist; it should be a haze of moisture, never leaving drops on the leaves. Rex begonias and other damp-lovers will do best if the gravel or pebbles in their saucers or trays is kept wet.

Begonias, achimenes and sinningias will all need to be kept damp and out of the sun. Remember, too, to give your plants as much fresh air as possible, and to keep their leaves clean and dust-free.

Another good way to help conserve humidity is to group plants together, perhaps on a tray of damp pebbles or in a deeper trough lined with damp peat. One plant which is much happier close to others than when standing alone is dizygotheca, sometimes sold as false aralia. This is not one of the easier plants to keep as it must be warm and humid (not below 12–16°C/54–61°F in winter), and likes a constant soil temperature of 18–20°C (64–68°F). Very moderate soft-water watering is enough in summer, and

very little in autumn and winter. It is a most beautiful plant, with jagged-edged leaves rather like hacksaw blades, bronzy copper when young turning to almost black, giving the plant one of the most fascinating silhouettes, almost like the finest cast iron. It must be sprayed all the year round and needs feeding every 2 weeks from March or April to the end of August; it looks good with the contrasting foliage of cyperus and dracaenas.

POSITION

Most flowering plants, except geraniums, do better out of direct sun – and you can appreciate the colours so much better if the light is not behind them. Remove finished flowers from the plant constantly so that you get more.

TAKING CUTTINGS

This is the best time of year to take cuttings of leaf cacti such as epiphyllums, which grow erect and flower in summer, and schlumbergera, the Christmas cactus, which is arching and trailing and flowers in autumn and winter. Rhipsalidopsis, known as the Easter cactus, is another arching and trailing plant, this one flowering in spring or early summer. Sections of the flattened leaf-like stems will root easily in sandy soil.

July and August are in fact the best months for taking cuttings in general, as plants should have a lot of healthy new growth at this time (see pp. 70–71 on taking cuttings).

Annuals and Outdoor Plants

FOOD PLANTS

Small tomato and capsicum plants will need regular feeding and lots of water; it is always exciting to see the first fruits appearing after the flowers, and the more you spray the more you will get to set. Even if you cannot produce a harvest festival on the window sill they make pretty plants, and it is a great pleasure to eat your own tomatoes with your own basil or parsley.

HERBS

The herbs on your kitchen window sill should have grown into sturdy little plants by July. You can cut and dry small bunches now; this will encourage further growth. Hang the bunches upside down in an airy place until the sprigs rattle in a dry way then rub between the palms and

DISH GARDENS

These miniature gardens can be very effective; small pebbles and rocks give them all the charm of small-scale Japanese gardens – a Lilliputian form of landscape gardening. Any shallow dish or trough can be used, but whatever it is it should not be less than 8–10 cm (3–4 in) deep, to give enough depth for a drainage layer of gravel at the bottom, with a little charcoal mixed in to keep it sweet. The water will evaporate more quickly from a shallow dish than from a pot, but moisture will be preserved by a layer of gravel on the surface, giving the right 'desert' look.

All the plants chosen have to share a liking for the same dry conditions and be relatively slow-growing. Cacti and succulents are the traditional choices as they will last happily for some years in a dish. Kalanchoe, small bromeliads, peperomias and small ivies will only last a year or so before they get overcrowded and

starved; they must therefore be potted on into bigger pots at this stage.

Any potting compost will do for cacti growing in a dish, but it should have sand or fine grit as one third of the mixture. Cacti must not be planted too close together; the spaces between plants are as important as the plants themselves in these designs. Some of the best groups will be those of one family, a collection of mammillarias for example, which flower easily in a sunny place, or columns of chamaecereus or of the 'rabbit's ears' opuntias, or a splendid example of a single, large, globular echinocereus. All these will be happy kept dry in winter in a cool place. Gasterias, aloes and echeverias are other good subjects for dish gardens.

Overwatering is fatal for all these, so, even more than with ordinary house-plants, it is best to give always less than you think.

WHAT CAN GO WRONG WITH YOUR PLANTS

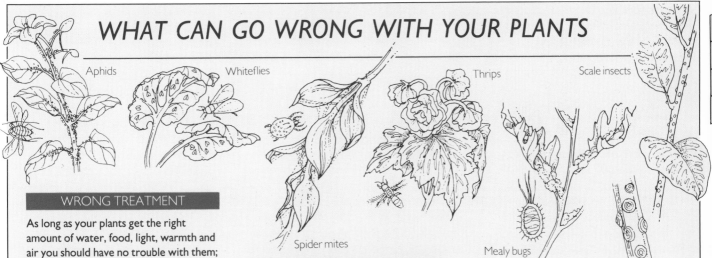

Aphids　　Whiteflies　　Thrips　　Scale insects

Spider mites　　Mealy bugs

WRONG TREATMENT

As long as your plants get the right amount of water, food, light, warmth and air you should have no trouble with them; diseases do not go round looking for a plant, they are caused by unhealthy conditions. Regular cleaning of the leaves is important; you should also look frequently at the soil ball in the pot to see there is no waterlogging and that the plant is not pot-bound, with roots escaping from the bottom. You should look carefully at any new plant to make sure it is healthy and not harbouring any unwelcome livestock.

Wilting and falling leaves can be a sign of over- or underwatering, usually the former. If the compost has got very dry immerse the pot in a bucket of water for 20 minutes, drain, and replace. If it is waterlogged take out the plant and root ball, remove as much as you can of the old compost, and repot in just moist compost.

Lack of vigour Sometimes a plant seems healthy enough but shows no signs of growth; repotting or potting on can often have almost miraculous effects and spur it on to strong growth.

Brown spots on leaves can be due to sun or heat burn. Move the plant to a more shaded place.

Thin pale growth is usually due to lack of light.

Yellow leaves can indicate a pot-bound condition, and sometimes overwatering.

Browning leaf edges The plant could be pot-bound, in too high or too low a temperature, or, again, it could be suffering from under- or overwatering.

Tall, lanky stems, particularly with geraniums, suggest that the plant has been flowering well but not given enough fertilizer, or that the plant was not cut back in spring or August. Cut stems down to about 23 cm (9 in).

PESTS

Apart from the above symptoms, which are caused by wrong treatment, there are, unfortunately, certain pests which occasionally make their presence known.

A pest may be one of many creeping, flying or crawling creatures, which aim to make your houseplants their home and nursery; they always make their way into the house from outside.

The larger pests are easy to spot and remove, and their traces, such as chewed leaves, are obvious. These are the slugs, snails and caterpillars, which are as a rule only found on plants in containers outside. It is a simple matter to remove these creatures, either by hand or with the use of slug bait or caterpillar spray.

It is the smaller, almost invisible, creatures which are the worst enemies, as they are often unsuspected and unseen until you become aware of the damage they are doing to the plant. These are mainly suckers, feeding from the plant juices; the most familiar are aphids (greenfly). Most are easily removed, severe attacks needing the use of a sprayed insecticide. This must be used with great care; spray outside if possible, and out of the way of children and pets.

Aphids can be green, black or brown, with or without wings, and usually accumulate on the undersides of leaves and young shoots, sometimes excreting a sticky substance called mildew which attracts ants. They are most common on plants outside. They can be washed off with a soapy solution sprayed on, wiped off with soaked cotton wool, or sprayed

with an insecticide. Aphids get in from outside in the summer, but they are easy to spot and deal with.

Whiteflies These are very small, often disturbed when the plant is moved. They settle on the undersides of leaves, multiplying at enormous speed. The leaves begin to look mottled, crumpled and unhealthy. Spray with insecticide.

Red spider mites These tiny creatures are not spiders at all; they only appear in extremely hot, dry conditions, and more often in greenhouses and conservatories than in the normal house (greenhouses can get very dry in the summer). Keeping plants well aired and frequently sprayed to keep up humidity will keep them away. Brown, shrivelled leaves in a very dry place are a sign that they are about. A soap solution or an insecticide spray will remove them.

Thrips are small, black, flying insects which feed on buds, leaves and flowers, leaving a silvery sheen and speckled marks. If you shake the plant over a sheet of newspaper they will drop off; again a soap solution or an insecticide spray will destroy them.

Mealy bugs are like tufts or specks of white cotton clustering under leaves. They can be removed by hand or with a pad of cotton wool soaked in alcohol (methylated spirits) or soapy water; if bad, spray with insecticide.

Scale insects denote their presence by a black, sticky deposit on stems and leaves. Again, remove by hand or cotton wool; if severe, spray with insecticide.

store the powder (not rubbed *too* fine) in airtight jars. This is the time to sow more basil and parsley for the autumn. Meanwhile, don't forget to water and feed your plants regularly.

FLOWERING PLANTS

Plants on sunny sills, and most of all in window boxes and hanging baskets, will need watering a lot, twice a day in really hot weather. And do not forget that the annual flowering plants will need feeding as well as generous watering.

Annuals must be dead-headed regularly if they are to keep on producing flowers. Their one idea is to set seed, so given the chance that is what they will do – in which case they won't need to bother to keep producing more flowers.

Plants to Buy

This is a good time to buy most pot plants; they are in good growth and will have three months or more to settle in to their new homes before the winter. Look out for the small tree-like crassulas, and other succulents like echevearias and the pale moon-like pachyphytums (both with a soft bloom on the leaves); they are all lovely summer plants and look just as good when taking their winter rest.

This is perhaps a good time to mention *Euphorbia milii*, the crown of thorns, one of my very favourite plants. Its tiny leaves are a bright mid-green, the jewel-like scarlet flowers (really bracts) are dotted along the thorny stems for most of the year, and the whole plant has a spare, angular quality about it. It grows to 60 cm (2 ft) high and is rather sprawling, but it can be kept neat by pruning (cuttings root well if allowed to callus or dry for 2 or 3 days before setting in gritty compost). Even in the winter, when it should be kept almost dry, it has some leaves and sometimes flowers showing. The yellowing and dropping of leaves in the autumn is quite normal, but at other times it can also be a sign of either over- or under-watering. *E. milii* is a plant which likes to bask in the hot summer sun. It needs a light place in winter too.

Being really provident and thinking ahead, people wanting special bulbs for winter flowering should order them now.

AUGUST

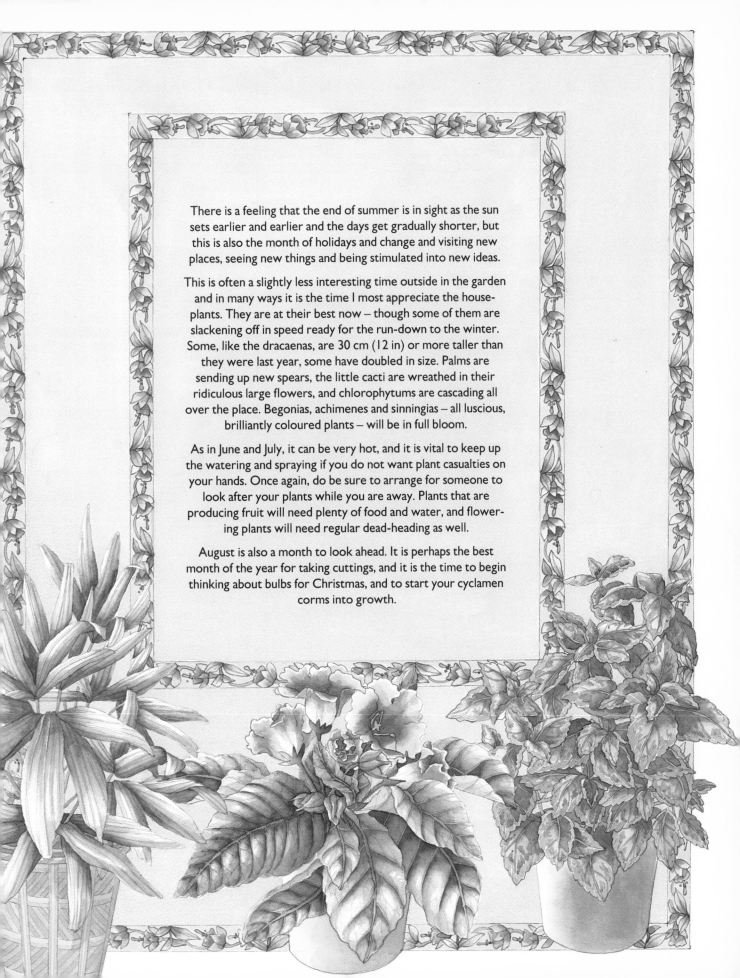

There is a feeling that the end of summer is in sight as the sun sets earlier and earlier and the days get gradually shorter, but this is also the month of holidays and change and visiting new places, seeing new things and being stimulated into new ideas.

This is often a slightly less interesting time outside in the garden and in many ways it is the time I most appreciate the house-plants. They are at their best now — though some of them are slackening off in speed ready for the run-down to the winter. Some, like the dracaenas, are 30 cm (12 in) or more taller than they were last year, some have doubled in size. Palms are sending up new spears, the little cacti are wreathed in their ridiculous large flowers, and chlorophytums are cascading all over the place. Begonias, achimenes and sinningias — all luscious, brilliantly coloured plants — will be in full bloom.

As in June and July, it can be very hot, and it is vital to keep up the watering and spraying if you do not want plant casualties on your hands. Once again, do be sure to arrange for someone to look after your plants while you are away. Plants that are producing fruit will need plenty of food and water, and flower-ing plants will need regular dead-heading as well.

August is also a month to look ahead. It is perhaps the best month of the year for taking cuttings, and it is the time to begin thinking about bulbs for Christmas, and to start your cyclamen corms into growth.

AUGUST

TO BUY

A GOOD TIME TO BUY MOST HOUSEPLANTS;
KEEP YOUR EYES OPEN FOR SHOWS AND FÊTES

CAMPANULA ISOPHYLLA NOW IN THE SHOPS

BUY SPRING BULBS FOR WINTER FLOWERING

IN FLOWER

MIMOSA AND *PUNICA GRANATUM* STARTING TO
FLOWER

**HYDRANGEA, REICHSTEINERIA, SAXIFRAGA
AND SPATHIPHYLLUM FINISHING**

ALL THE OTHER SUMMER FLOWERS STILL IN FULL
BLOOM, INDOORS AND OUT

**MOST CACTI AND SUCCULENTS PRODUCING
FLOWERS NOW AND IN JULY**

OUTSIDE CALLUNA HEATHERS BEGINNING TO
FLOWER

**AUBERGINES, BEANS, CHILLIES, PEPPERS, AND
TOMATOES FRUITING**

1. Ipomoea
2. Petunia
3. Begonia tuberhybrida
4. Fuchsia
5. Rhapsis excelsa
6. Sinningia speciosa
7. Coleus blumei

Looking After Your Houseplants

WATERING, FEEDING, HUMIDITY

The usual summer rules apply: water your plants generously and spray frequently to keep the humidity right. Ferns, palms and arums, although not in the sun, will be feeling the warmth and will need constant spraying. But you should be beginning to slacken off the feeding, unless plants are in very strong growth. Give less food, probably leaving an extra week between feeds, until you are giving nothing at all except to winter-flowering plants.

Plants have to be left some time, and the best way to ensure their well-being is to have a reliable friend who can be trusted not to forget to water them or to drown them in an excess of watering. Failing this there are various ways of keeping plants happy for a week or so while you are away on holiday.

First of all they should be put in a cool, light place away from the sun to conserve all the water they can. Small plants can be watered and put in a plastic bag tied loosely over the plant with a small air hole, with the plastic held off the leaves by canes; this should keep them in good health for about 3 weeks. Larger plants can be put in a bowl or bath of water 5–8 cm (2–3 in) deep – if in a bath stand them on mats or cloths so as not to scratch the enamel. You can buy a special matting for this called capillary matting, which holds 1 litre (1¾ pints) of water to the square metre (yard); you can line the bath with this and leave the tap very slightly dripping. Again there are special water dispensers which you stick in the pot and which let a regulated amount of water through.

If you are a very busy person who has somehow accumulated some indoor plants, or you have to be away from them a lot, you may wish to make use of self-watering containers for them (see p. 27 for details).

If you do have to leave the plants for a holiday it is likely that a number of them will need a good soak in a bucket of water when you come back.

CHECKING FOR PESTS

As the windows will be open a lot watch out for pests like greenfly; the regular spraying should ensure that red spider mite will not appear as it thrives only in dry heat.

STARTING PLANTS INTO GROWTH

If you have kept a cyclamen corm dry since the spring you can put it into damp compost in a shady place now and hope for flowers in the winter.

You could also put hyacinth or daffodil bulbs in a bowl for flowers in December (see p. 77 for planting instructions).

TAKING CUTTINGS

August is the best month for taking and striking cuttings, as most plants are then at the peak of their growth, although any time in the summer will do for this. Shrubby plants like rosemary, sage, thyme and winter savory take well now (see pp. 70–71 for instructions).

Many of your geraniums and pelargoniums may well almost have finished flowering now, and they will most likely be looking very untidy and straggly; give them a good prune to get them into shape for their winter rest and pop the cuttings of any you particularly like into a pot of sandy compost to root. But if they still have lots of flowers, and are producing new buds, let them carry on – often until October or November.

Ever since Victorian times the plants which are happy in the relatively low light of rooms have been the most successful indoor plants; the best and most long-lasting of these are from the shady rain forests of the tropics. The Araceae, or arum family, includes a number of the perennially popular houseplants; they are happy in a normal living room temperature, providing the humidity is kept generous, and they enjoy being grown in groups where they can make their own micro-climate. If you are starting with indoor plants a collection of these, growing together, in a damp, gravel-filled trough or tray, would make a good beginning.

Dieffenbachias or dumb canes Their upright-growing leaves are often speckled in a white, yellow or green pattern. They need warm, dampish conditions, a little extra peat to add moisture if you are using a loam-based compost, and sand for drainage. A temperature of about 20°C (68°F) will suit them, but they do not mind a lower one in winter (15–16°C/59–61°F) when of course they will need less water. Liberal feeding and water in summer and a good light place will keep them happy.

Monstera deliciosa, the Swiss cheese plant, must be one of the best known houseplants. When it is really happy it can grow into a plant 3 m (10 ft) high, as it is a tree climber back at home in the Mexican jungles. Give it a free-draining potting mixture with added grit or Perlite; ready-made peat composts are suitable as long as they are not allowed to become waterlogged. It likes a good light, but not direct sunlight; it should be kept at 20°C (68°F), but is tough enough to live at 10°C (50°F). The large leaves should be wiped free of dust and sprayed frequently.

Philodendrons There are several varieties of these; one of the best for rooms is *P. scandens*, the sweetheart vine, as it is

practically indestructible as long as it is reasonably warm. It has heart-shaped leaves and can be trained to climb or trail. Other philodendrons to try are *P. elegans*, which is also a climber with fingered, palm-like leaves; *P. bipinnatifidum*, with deep green, incised leaves; and *P. erubescens*, with long, spear-shaped leaves, rose-coloured when young.

Aglaonema, the Chinese evergreen, comes from South-east Asia. It has pointed leaves, and makes a bushy plant up to 45 cm (18 in) high. Normal living room temperatures are ideal, not going below 13°C (55°F) at night. A shady place is best.

Syngonium has glossy green arrow-shaped leaves. These plants either trail or climb up moss poles. Light shade is best and normal temperatures, preferably not below 16°C (61°F). Spray foliage frequently.

Scindapsus is another easily grown climber from the Pacific rain forests. It tolerates low light and is happy climbing moss poles. The temperature in winter should not go below 16°C (61°F). Like all its cousins it likes a lot of spraying, and its pot should stand on damp gravel or pebbles, or in a tray of damp peat.

Moss poles for these jungle climbers can be bought at indoor plant centres.

PROPAGATION TIPS

Seeds
Last good month for houseplants and perennial herbs.

Cuttings
Best month, and the traditional month, for all cuttings; good month for potting offsets.

Bulbs
Cyclamen should be repotted; hyacinths and daffodils can be planted.

VARIOUS WAYS OF PROPAGATING PLANTS

WHEN TO TAKE CUTTINGS

Leaf and stem cuttings are best taken in the summer months, as the plants are in full healthy growth, and there must be enough of the plant to give up the odd leaf or stem. August is the traditional month for this, but any time between April and August should do.

In fact leaf cuttings can be taken at any time as long as a temperature of around 20°C (68°F) and sufficient humidity can be provided. All you need is a box of compost with a lid, or a pot covered with a plastic dome or a clear polythene bag – anything which makes in effect a miniature warm greenhouse. Some plants like tradescantia, impatiens, cyperus, hedera (ivy) and heptapleurum, which root very easily in compost or water, can also be rooted at any time.

TAKING LEAF CUTTINGS

Leaf cuttings are traditionally taken in August; the plants are in full and healthy growth, and a window sill with a glass or plastic topped pot will give the right temperature.

African violets (saintpaulia) and the smaller-leaved peperomias and begonias are propagated from single leaves with about 5 cm (2 in) of stem; they should be set 2.5 cm (1 in) deep in rooting mixture (damp sand and peat) (see p. 10 for details). The plastic-lidded propagator trays for raising seeds are ideal for this.

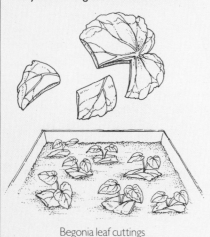

Begonia leaf cuttings

Larger leaves like those of the dramatic *Begonia rex* and *Peperomia argyreia* are cut into small pieces (2.5 cm/1 in or so square), placed on the rooting mixture vein side down, and held in place by hairpins, unbent paper clips, or small stones. Alternatively they can be left intact, laid on the surface with the vein intersections cut or nicked with a knife, and held lightly down as above. Small plants should appear where the vein incisions have been made.

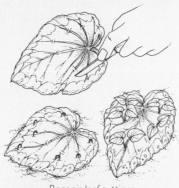

Begonia leaf cuttings

Easiest of all are the long, narrow leaves of succulents like leaf cacti and sansevierias. The leaves are cut into 5–8 cm (2–3 in) sections and inserted into the compost (bottom side down).

Small plants should root in 1–6 weeks from all these methods, and when well rooted they must be potted up. Lift them carefully and set the tiny plants in peat-based compost in small pots (yoghurt or cream cartons will do very well if you make a drainage hole in the bottom). They should then be put back in the propagator box for 2 or 3 weeks to make sure they form more roots and become strong.

Leaf cuttings of succulents and cacti

STEM, TIP AND BASAL CUTTINGS

Some easy plants to take cuttings from are tradescantia, zebrina, setcreasea, cyperus, hedera (ivy), and impatiens (busy lizzie), which root easily either in water or in a mixture of compost and sand or grit. I have found that schefflera and heptapleurum also root well in water. I have a large bushy heptapleurum which started off as a stem cutting from a friend 9 months ago.

Always remove the cutting from the parent plant by cutting just above a node. Then make a clean cut with a sharp knife or secateurs just below a node (joint) in the stem and remove the lower leaves. The cut just below a node should be in the soil, as this is where the cutting roots. Young healthy stems naturally give the best and healthiest cuttings; they can be anything from 8 cm (3 in) to 23 cm (9 in) long. If you are rooting your cutting in water it is a good idea to put a piece of charcoal in the jar to keep the water sweet; when the roots appear put the new plant into your compost mix.

Sand is an excellent rooting medium, or an equal mix of sand or grit and potting compost. You can dip the stems first into a hormone rooting powder to help quick rooting (though I must admit I always forget to buy this and have so far managed quite well without).

Most cuttings root best in a humid environment; a clear plastic bag held up with small canes over the pot will provide this, or there are the plastic propagating trays with lids and pots with clear plastic domes. Generally speaking most cuttings are happy to root at 16–18°C (61–64°F). Whether you will need a heated propagator or just a warm sill depends on the time of year. Some cuttings, like geraniums, root easily by just being pushed into damp compost.

The main difference between stem and tip cuttings is that tip cuttings are more green, less woody, with more new growth. Tip cuttings will always have a growing point, but stem cuttings will often have one too, although they need not. Geraniums root well from pieces of

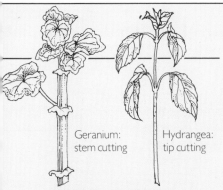

Geranium: stem cutting   Hydrangea: tip cutting

stem without a growing point; hydrangeas root well from young tip cuttings.

Basal cuttings are shoots growing out of a main stem, often near the base; the shoots that are used as cuttings will therefore be unwanted growth, as the main stem should be clear of side-shoots.

Taking basal cuttings

LAYERING

Layering is used when there are long flexible stems which can be bent down, nicked on the underside with a sharp knife, and pegged into a pot of compost, while still joined to the parent plant. A cut-off stem can also be rooted in the same way if you are reasonably quick about it and keep the cutting damp before potting. Ivies and *Ficus pumila* root well like this.

Layering

AIR LAYERING

This is a bit more complicated; the technique is usually used when you have a tall plant which is too big, or which has too much bare stem. A new plant is made from a long stem; dracaena, cordyline, and varieties of *Ficus elastica* (rubber plant) are the commonest plants to experience this. You choose your length of stem and make an incision halfway through the stem where you want the new roots to form. Brush the cut with hormone rooting powder and keep it open with a match stick or similar slip of wood. Put a length of polythene round the stem 8–10 cm (3–4 in) below the base of the cut, and attach it with sticky tape to the stem (so that it looks like a floppy wineglass). Pack this floppy wineglass with a mixture of moist sphagnum moss and peat-based compost and tie or tape it round the top 8–10 cm (3–4 in) above the cut. You now have a plump plastic bundle or bandage.

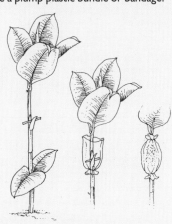

Air layering

After about 2 months you should see roots through the plastic; cut the stem below the bundle, carefully remove the plastic, and pot the new, shorter, plant. Keep the bare stem that is left as it may well shoot too and you will then have two plants.

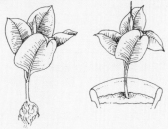

DIVISION

Many plants form a mass of roots, and you can only go on potting up for so long. These roots can be divided easily when they get too big, and the beginning of the growing season is usually the best time for this. Knock the plant out of the pot, pull the roots apart into two or three sections, and pot them up separately. Aspidistra, chlorophytum, and maranta are among the plants divided like this.

Dividing a clump of roots

PROPAGATION FROM OFFSETS

Some plants very obligingly produce offsets (or offshoots) which can be cut off with a knife and potted separately into small pots to grow on; these are small replicas or babies of the parent plant which develop close to it. Chlorophytums produce their offsets in great profusion at the end of their long flowering stems; bromeliad rosettes normally die after flowering, but several young offsets are produced long before this happens and can be removed and planted when they are about a quarter the size of the original rosette. Aloes also send up young plants from the base which can grow on with the parent plant until the pot gets too crowded. Kalanchoe produces offsets along the leaf edges. Offsets can be removed and potted separately any time from March or April until September or October.

Propagation from offsets

Annuals and Outdoor Plants

FOOD PLANTS

Plants that are producing fruit, as many should be now, will need a lot of water and food, while spraying will encourage the beans and little tomatoes to set fruit. It is worth repeating that the spray should be in use every day, as plants take in water through their leaves as well as their roots, and a dry atmosphere encourages red spider mite.

FLOWERING PLANTS

If you have planted ipomoeas in a window box or in pots they will be at the top of their canes or strings by now and twining round themselves, covered in flowers. Do remember to dead-head the morning glories; they only last a day, but the flowers are large and vivid blue and quite beautiful. Spraying will also encourage them to produce new flowers. Remember that all annuals will need plenty of food and water, and regular dead-heading if they are to continue to flower. Roses also need dead-heading.

HERBS

This is really the last month for sowing seed, either of perennials like winter savory, thyme and chives or of annuals like parsley and basil for winter supplies. It is also a good time to take cuttings of the shrubby herbs: rosemary, sage, thyme and winter savory. And you should of course carry on cutting and drying herbs for the winter.

Plants to Buy

If you are out and about this month keep an eye out for shows and fêtes – often good places for buying plants. August is a good month for buying houseplants; many of my favourites have been acquired at local shows and jumble sales as tiny potted offsets – the Women's Institutes are particularly good at these.

A cheering plant to look out for is *Campanula isophylla*, which flowers from late summer to the end of the autumn, when it is rested by cutting back the stems and putting it in a cool place. The bell flowers are pale blue or white and densely cover the trailing stems.

As we must, sadly, think about the winter, buy some hyacinth or daffodil bulbs to put in a bowl, and you should have spring flowers in December.

SOILLESS OR HYDROPONIC PLANT GROWING

Indoor plant growing gets further and further from good old-fashioned earth. First we had the light, clean, easy peat-based mixtures, and now plants can be grown in water. Hydroponics, which means literally 'water work', is a growing system, only readily available in this country in the last 10 years, which uses a sterile soil substitute, usually porous clay granules, to hold the plant up, and a water and nutrient solution to give it all it needs.

Only in the last hundred years has it been understood that the roots of a plant do not in some mysterious manner 'eat' the soil. Roots have three main functions: they take in nutrients from the soil, they absorb oxygen from the air spaces in the soil, and they keep the plant firmly anchored upright.

Most systems for hydroculture consist of two containers, an outer one of plastic and a free-draining inner one filled with clay granules. Water with fertilizer is added to the outer container, which has a gauge to indicate the correct level. This means that the old problem of how much or how little water to give no longer exists, and as it is perfectly clean the risk of pests and disease disappears as well. The normal essentials for healthy plants – the right temperature, light and humidity – of course remain the same. Plant growth is usually faster and lusher than in a compost mixture, so plants tend to become top-heavy and need more frequent pruning. Plants sold in these special pots are also more expensive than those in

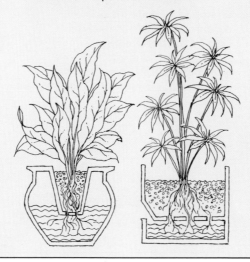

more traditional compost; they come complete with instructions, and you only need to top up the water to the correct level and add the nutrients. Not all plants take to this way of growing – cissus, coleus, some palms, philodendrons and ivies are some that do. The roots become thicker than normal, so plants cannot be changed from this method to compost or vice versa.

You can also buy hydropots in several sizes, with a water store base in which the nutrient is poured on to the granules rather than added to the water. Generally speaking the plants need feeding only once or twice a year by this method. This system is most suitable for offices and public places.

When plants outgrow their original pots it is not because they are 'pot-bound' in the traditional sense (roots filling the compost in the pot) but because the plant itself gets too large to be held up by the clay granules. Water must always be at room temperature, and the fertilizers those specially designed for hydroculture.

SEPTEMBER

September, the harvest month. Much though I hate to admit the fact, this is the first month of autumn; the days are getting shorter, there is a freshness and briskness in the air, and the sunshine seems almost unnaturally bright. There is everywhere an air of sad acceptance. September seems to me in a way complementary to March; its immediate opposite in the circle of months, you get the same winds and showers and shining, rain-washed sunny spells, clouds moving fast in a bright sky, every shadow intensifying the brightness, every leaf highlighted.

The change in season is very much reflected in the care of your plants. As growth begins to slow down, you should start to give plants less water and food. You should be thinking about suitable winter positions for your plants, clearing window boxes and hanging baskets as the annuals die down, and planting bulbs to flower around Christmas and the New Year. With so many plants still in flower both indoors and out, planting spring bulbs may seem a pretty remote bit of advance planning. By the time they flower, however, all the begonias, campanulas, sin-ningias, roses and geraniums will be over, and outside there may well be nothing except winter-flowering heathers. The delicate flowers, the sweet scent, and the suggestion of spring that these bulbs bring will then be greatly appreciated. All this brings home to one the sad truth that summer is over and autumn has arrived.

SEPTEMBER

TO BUY

GOOD TIME FOR BUYING ALL HOUSEPLANTS

PLANTS TO FLOWER IN WINDOW BOXES IN SPRING – ALSO DWARF EVERGREENS AND WINTER-FLOWERING HEATHERS

SPRING BULBS FOR INSIDE AND OUT

IN FLOWER

CAPSICUMS AND ARDISIA BEGINNING TO FRUIT

MANY SUMMER-FLOWERING PLANTS FINISHING: ABUTILON, ACHIMENES, TUBEROUS-ROOTED BEGONIAS, BELOPERONE, BROWALLIA, BRUNFELSIA, CROSSANDRA, FUCHSIA, HOYA, MIMOSA, *PUNICA GRANATUM*, SINNINGIA

STILL FLOWERING ARE CANE-STEMMED BEGONIAS, *CAMPANULA ISOPHYLLA, EXACUM AFFINE*, HIBISCUS, IPOMOEA, PELARGONIUMS, ROSES, *STEPHANOTIS FLORIBUNDA*, STREPTOCARPUS, THUNBERGIA

AUBERGINES, BEANS, CHILLIES, PEPPERS AND TOMATOES FRUITING

1	Tomatoes
2	Chives
3	Basil
4	Rosemary
5	Parsley
6	Croton
7	Croton
8	Capsicum annuum
9	Ananas comosus
10	Avocado

Looking After Your Houseplants

WATERING

The days may seem to be almost summer-like, but the houseplants can tell the difference. Many plants begin to go into their dormant, resting season about now, so watering should be gradually less and less.

Very often at this time of year plants will have yellowing or drooping leaves. This is not a sign of interior autumn but could well be the result of over-enthusiastic watering. Any plants showing these symptoms must be allowed to dry out completely before moderate watering is begun again.

FEEDING

By the end of this month you should have stopped feeding all your plants except the winter-flowering ones. Arums such as *Monstera deliciosa* and the philodendrons, the various species of ficus, and the dracaenas have all, or *should* have all, been fed every fortnight since April or May and now have to get their rest so as to gain strength for next year. It may be tempting to go on feeding plants such as arums, as they seem so full of vigour, but they do need the winter rest.

Stop feeding hippeastrums, too, and let the leaves die down.

HUMIDITY

For those plants that need it, such as ferns, humidity should be kept up as in the previous months, unless it is very cool. The cooler it is the less necessary it is – though, of course, plants that spend the winter in warm, centrally heated rooms will need the humidity just as much as they did in the hot, dry days of summer.

POSITION

As the plants begin to slow down this is an ideal time to plan out their autumn and winter quarters, as many must have a cooler place to rest in than the normal living room, which would be too warm and set them off growing again, or in some cases dry them up fatally. Ferns are among these, as they cannot stand dry conditions; auracaria, the Norfolk Island pine, also needs a cool spot. Most dracaenas, schefflera, heptapleurum and *Ficus benjamina*, the weeping fig, prefer it less warm if possible, and ivies, azaleas, chamaedorea, *Cissus antarctica*, fatsia and tradescantia will also be happier somewhere where the temperature does not go above 5–15°C (41–59°F). Some plants need less light than others in winter; the howea or kentia palm, cyrtomium the holly fern, and *Monstera deliciosa* will all be content away from a window.

Aspidistras and rex begonias will be happy in a bathroom in winter if there is enough light, as will the ferns. The good old cast iron aspidistra which decorated many a Victorian parlour, not minding the gas fumes and relishing the cool, is a lovely plant and looks very handsome if kept clean and shiny. Most of the time I have mine in a darkish, north-facing window. It never gets any food as this tends to make the large leaves split. Sometimes it decorates the bathroom, covering some pipes, where there is hardly any light at all.

Be sure you find a cool, bright place for your cacti and succulents to winter in. On the whole these are small plants and you can pack a number of them on a large meat dish or tray.

Geraniums and fuchsias should also be put in a cool, light place. Do not forget to give them modest amounts of water throughout the winter.

Plants which like a lot of light can be put into a sunny window, but some of the tender ones must be removed from cold windows, particularly at night.

So, although you do not have to move your plants just yet, this is the moment to start working out new placings, and to try

SPRING BULBS

This month is the crucial time for bulb planting; flowering bulbs are the easiest as well as the most welcome of temporary houseplants. The bulbs for sale now have been specially prepared by the growers to come into flower round about Christmas and the New Year, and when you have bought them it is as well to plant them as soon as possible. You can also buy ordinary bulbs for planting outside in window boxes or other containers to flower in the spring.

The favourites, and rightly so, are hyacinths, and the different varieties of narcissus, including the dancing daffodils. Others to consider are snowdrops, grape hyacinths, tulips, large-flowered crocuses, scillas, dwarf irises, and chionodoxa – all these will make lovely temporary houseplants.

PLANTING AND LOOKING AFTER THEM

Spring bulbs can be grown in any proprietary compost mixture, or in a special bulb fibre. Two or three small pieces of charcoal in the bowl will keep the compost sweet and avoid stagnation. Whatever the growing medium it must be moistened before use; put a layer in the bowl, firm it lightly, and then place the bulbs in it so that their tops are level with or just above the rim. Put them close together without touching and stand them gently in – never screw them in – then put the rest of the soil mix round them. When planting small bulbs like crocuses and small tulips you cover them completely, while larger bulbs should have their tips showing.

After planting, the bowls or pots must be put in a cool, dark place, if possible below 9°C (48°F), as this will encourage root growth. A dark cupboard will do, and you can put newspaper over them or enclose them completely in a black plastic bag, as they should be as dark and as cool as possible. Check from time to time to make sure they are not drying out and water them if necessary. In 4–8 weeks the bulbs will shoot; when these shoots are 2.5 cm (1 in) long put the pots or bowls into a lighter place for 7–10 days, after which they can go into a bright light at a temperature of 16°C (61°F). When the leaves are fully grown and the flower buds showing they can be moved into their final living room quarters. Keep the compost *moist*, not wet.

Large bulbs can also be grown singly in water in special glass containers. These are also started in semi-darkness or complete darkness in early autumn, with a few pieces of charcoal in the water. Crocus and small narcissus bulbs are also sometimes grown in trays of pebbles and water. The bulbs are wedged into the pebbles and the tray topped up with water. You can also plant the smaller spring-flowering bulbs such as scillas, grape hyacinths, dwarf iris and snowdrops in clay pans.

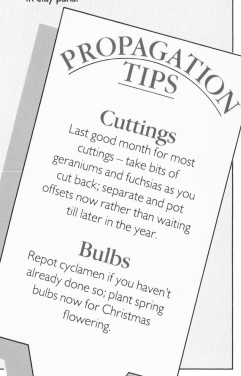

PROPAGATION TIPS

Cuttings

Last good month for most cuttings – take bits of geraniums and fuchsias as you cut back; separate and pot offsets now rather than waiting till later in the year.

Bulbs

Repot cyclamen if you haven't already done so; plant spring bulbs now for Christmas flowering.

plants in different situations; their growth will not be checked as they are beginning to rest anyway. Most plants are happiest undisturbed as long as the situation suits them, but you can experiment by moving them as long as you remember their light requirements. If any of your plants have been enjoying a summer outside, don't forget that they, too, will need suitable indoor winter quarters.

TIDYING UP YOUR PLANTS

Geraniums, pelargoniums and fuchsias are some of the houseplants that may look very untidy and straggly by this time of year, and need tidying up before their winter rest. Cut them back to a good shape, and remove any dead leaves. Foliage begonias and myrtle may also need a tidy-up.

CHECKING FOR PESTS

Sometimes at this time of year whitefly can appear on plants which have been on sills, small clouds of them flying up when the leaves are disturbed. Pelargoniums, geraniums and sparmannias seem especially prone to this pest. They are easily dealt with by the use of an insecticide spray, so spray at once before they get on to the leaves of other plants.

The dreaded red spider mite often makes its presence felt now too; yellowing, twisting leaves and fine webs are the things to look out for. These must be dealt with at once with a suitable spray. It is only in very dry conditions that these pests can survive so keeping up the humidity round plants, especially in warm places, should keep them at bay.

REPOTTING

Have a careful look at all the houseplants to see whether any obviously need repotting, with roots appearing through the drainage holes at the base of the pot; if so do it this month, or early in October at the very latest.

AS PLANTS DIE DOWN

Sinningias, tuberous begonias and achimenes, which have been such a delight all the summer, will now begin to droop and die down ready for their winter rest. I usually put them in a cool corner, removing the dead stems when they pull off easily, and store the pots, dry, on their sides through the winter. They can then be repotted and started into growth again in spring.

Annuals and Outdoor Plants

FOOD PLANTS

Beans, tomatoes, peppers and other food plants will probably still be producing fruit, but they must all be cleared away as they finish. Never leave finished plants in pots or containers outside, even if you are going to leave them empty through the winter. Nothing looks more depressing than yellowing, dying leaves, and they can lead to disease.

HERBS

These can still be picked and dried, and you could still try sowing parsley and basil if you haven't done so yet. And it is not too late to take cuttings of the shrubby perennial herbs.

FLOWERING PLANTS

Many of the annual flowering plants like the gorgeous morning glory will be over now and must be thrown away.

As soon as your window boxes have been cleared you can plant sweet williams, forget-me-nots and sweet-scented wallflowers to flower early next summer – also polyanthus, primroses,

lily-of-the-valley, and pansies. These could be a background for crocuses or small tulips; red tulips and forget-me-nots are a traditional and pretty combination. Both crocuses and tulips also look good against the varying colours of dwarf evergreens. You could also plant winter-flowering heathers.

Plants to Buy

September is one of the best times to buy new houseplants as they will have enough time to get used to their new home before the winter but are not at the height of their growth. It is a good idea to give any new plants a thorough soak in a bucket of water, and then drain them, before putting them into their places.

Ardisia and capsicums should be just appearing in the shops now. There are also many plants available now for window boxes, such as wallflowers, sweet williams, and forget-me-nots, as well as winter-flowering heathers and dwarf evergreens.

It is also the time to buy spring bulbs, either to plant outside in boxes and pots or to flower in the house around Christmas and the New Year.

OCTOBER

Golden autumn, the season of mists and mellow fruitfulness, a
month of exciting winds and exuberant skies. Often this is the
most beautiful month of the year as the trees erupt in red and
gold in their last grand show before the leaves fall. It can be
sunny and warm during the day, the air crisp at night, the moon
and stars bright, the sun low across the landscape. Sometimes
the frosts come unexpectedly. A strange time of change, particularly when it comes to turning the clocks back and the darker
evenings put us squarely back into autumn. This is surely the
worst thing about October: one day we might be experiencing
almost an Indian summer, then suddenly it is dark at five o'clock.
Oh dear!

Though some of your summer plants may still be flowering –
some geraniums and begonias perhaps – the emphasis this
month is on preparing for winter. You should be giving the
plants much less water, and only those plants that flower in
winter should be getting any food. Plants that have spent the
summer outside should be brought in, and inside the houseplants will have to be moved into their winter positions. Some
will need to be cut back and generally tidied up. It is the last
month for repotting, for putting plants in the window boxes to
flower next spring, and for planting spring bulbs. Meanwhile the
seed catalogues start to come out, and plants like poinsettias
and solanums (winter cherry), which one associates so totally
with winter, appear in the shops.

OCTOBER

TO BUY

STILL A GOOD TIME TO BUY HOUSEPLANTS

SOLANUM AND POINSETTIAS NOW APPEARING IN SHOPS

· SPRING BULBS STILL IN SHOPS

SEED CATALOGUES APPEARING

IN FLOWER

APHELANDRA SQUARROSA AND POINSETTIA STARTING TO FLOWER

MOST OF THE SUMMER FLOWERS COMING TO AN END NOW: CANE-STEMMED BEGONIAS AND PERHAPS A FEW GERANIUMS STILL FLOWERING

ARDISIA, CAPSICUMS AND SOLANUMS FRUITING

OUTSIDE ERICA HEATHERS BEGINNING TO FLOWER

1 Cordyline terminalis
2 Vriesia poelmannii
3 Guzmania lingulata
4 Vriesia splendens
5 Aphelandra squarrosa
6 Sansevieria trifasciata
7 Chrysanthemum morifolium
8 Solanum capsicastrum

Looking After Your Houseplants

WATERING, FEEDING, HUMIDITY

Most of the plants will now need much less water, and feeding should have stopped unless growth is obviously going on.

One exception to this is the Christmas cactus, which should be forming its flower buds now. If you keep it moist, spray it regularly, and feed it once a week, you should have flowers all the winter.

Mist-spraying to keep up humidity is doubly important in warm rooms with little fresh air, particularly if you have central heating, which creates a very dry atmosphere.

POSITION

Perhaps you did all your plant moving for the winter last month; if not shift them about now. Some may be coming into the house after a summer outside on a balcony or in a window box, and these will benefit from a soak in a bucket of tepid water.

As fires are lit and central heating is turned on it will be obvious that some of the plants have to be moved. Palms and ferns, for example, had to be found positions out of the sun for the summer, but they could now go near a window.

Cacti and succulents should be put into their cool winter positions now, away from the sills where they have been sunbathing. They will be best in an unheated room, but wherever they are keep them as cool as possible. They will need only the barest drop of water in winter, once a month perhaps if they are in a place with the minimum of heat.

Some plants like geraniums may well still be looking good and enjoying the last warm, sunny days of the year; they

FREE PLANTS FROM PIPS AND STONES

Some of the most satisfying of indoor plants are those which have not cost you a penny, or only a very few pence, such as you might find at jumble sales. These can be plants nurtured from cuttings and seeds you acquire from friends, or plants which grow from by-products of things you have anyway and usually throw away, like pips and stones.

You can try planting an avocado stone, an orange pip, a peanut, or whatever, at any time of year, and just see what happens. October seems a nice time to start growing something new as so many plants have gone into hibernation for the winter.

This, incidentally, is a lovely way of getting children interested in growing things. Somewhere in Wiltshire now is a considerable sized chestnut tree which appeared in a flower pot where a conker was placed by a child in autumn, and a beautiful room in Oxfordshire houses a large lemon tree which started life as an accidental seedling on a compost heap in north London!

Avocados I suppose there is no doubt that the most popular 'free' plants are avocados grown from stones; there is a fascination and magic about the neat stones splitting and showing their tender purplish shoots and bronzy young leaves. I frequently start them off like this, but must admit that when large they are not my favourite plants, owing to their tendency to brown leaves and their slightly inelegant form. The large stones can be started into growth in damp peaty soil in a flower pot kept warm and moist or in water, with struts or supports of pins or toothpicks inserted and resting on the edge of a jar or glass with the base of the stone in water. If you use the water rooting method roots should form in a month or two, whereupon the rooted stone is ready to be transferred into sandy soil.

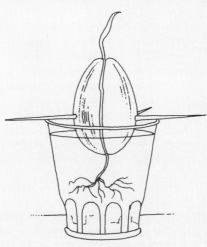

Avocado stone

Lychees, mangoes and loquats all grow from stones in the same way, making pretty little indoor trees that like moist conditions. Growth can take 2 or 3 months to start, but once started it is rapid: the lychee is capable of making almost 2 m (7 ft) of leafy stem in a year, and the mango grows nearly as tall, with contorted stems and long elegant leaves.

Peanuts, date palms Peanuts make small vine-like plants, and even date stones, if fresh, can produce date palms from a blade-like leaf in time, although patience is needed as they are slow-growing and need a lot of warmth.

Citrus plants The pips of all the citrus fruits – orange, lemon, grapefruit, lime and tangerine – should all germinate in moist compost if they are kept warm and dark. When the seedlings are 10 cm (4 in) tall put them into individual pots and they should grow well, needing potting on every year. All these make neat, small, shiny-leaved bushes, the tangerine being

the most lush. All are tender and must never get frosted; 8–10°C (46–50°F) suits them, and they will be happy on a sunny sill or outdoors in summer.

Native trees It is fun for children to plant an acorn or a conker to produce in time a small oak or chestnut; a walnut, sycamore seeds, or a pine nut from a pine cone will also produce shoots with luck. Walnuts and hazelnuts are best planted in sand in autumn, left in a cool place, and transplanted to compost in spring.

Fruit trees Apple, pear and plum trees can also be grown; the pips or stones should be put in the fridge in damp cotton wool until shoots appear and then put into pots. Plum stones should be very slightly cracked with nutcrackers first, as should those of peach, nectarine and apricot. These last three, unlike apple, pear and plum, will need a warm place to germinate, in 10 cm (4 in) pots of moist compost. As the little trees grow and are fed and repotted every year in spring you may get blossom but, sadly, no fruit.

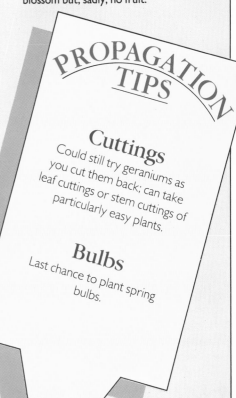

PROPAGATION TIPS

Cuttings
Could still try geraniums as you cut them back; can take leaf cuttings or stem cuttings of particularly easy plants.

Bulbs
Last chance to plant spring bulbs.

should be left where they are to finish flowering before being given their tidy-up and hair-cut. I have had them looking bright and beautiful as late as December. Make sure you have earmarked a cool, light place for their winter home, with the fuchsias and cacti, and keep them neat with dead leaves removed.

The most important thing to remember when choosing winter positions for your plants is that all the temperatures given in the Glossary for individual plants are the broad maximum and minimum: most plants are very tolerant, and a little above or below will not be disastrous; a plant may do *best* at something between 15 and 20°C (59–68°F), and need a winter minimum of 10°C (50°F) to grow slowly or just tick over, but still *survive* in a dormant state at anything above 5°C (41°F). In general a constant 18–21°C (64–70°F) is satisfactory for most plants sold for the house; humidity must be adequate at the top end of this scale, as the warmer it is the damper the air needs to be.

REPOTTING

October is the very last month for repotting, so look carefully to see if any plants have outgrown their pots and pot on quickly if they are pot-bound. (See p. 35 for step-by-step instructions.)

CHECKING FOR PESTS

Tidy plants up by removing dead leaves and keep a look out for pests like whitefly, which seem to be particularly fond of geraniums and pelargoniums. If plants have been in warm, dry conditions keep an eye out for the red spider mite, too. This will advertise its presence by fine webs and twisted leaves; spray affected plants with an insecticide such as melathion.

BROMELIADS

Some of the most dramatically shaped and architectural of indoor plants are the bromeliads, and these members of the pineapple family are among the most amenable and least demanding of houseplants to grow.

Most of them come from Central and South America, where they grow on the trunks and branches of trees or on the forest floor. Their other name, 'air pines', refers to their amazing ability to grow high up in the trees as epiphytes, needing no great depth of soil. Some grow on the ground in deserts, too, and it is this ability to adapt to various conditions that makes them good houseplants. They are not parasites, taking nourishment from a host plant, however, for they manage to get enough food for themselves from dead leaves caught in the angle of the branches. Most grow in the form of a rosette, the stiff leaves overlapping to form a small hollow or cup in the centre in which rain and dew form a reservoir of water for the plants in dry weather; this often serves as a bathing pool for tree frogs, too.

The majority of these plants flower once from each rosette, and when this has happened the plant dies and small offsets are produced round the base of the parent. As these plants are very slow-growing and the flowers last a long time the plants which are sold in flower will be good value for quite a while.

Being used to fissures in trees, bromeliads have shallow roots and most do well in small pots of well-drained compost; coarse peat and sharp sand or leaf mould and peat are suitable. They need a lot of water when growing, but like to

dry out before the next watering; the centre cup should be kept filled, the water being poured out and replaced from time to time. In summer give them a feed every fortnight and keep them in a good light; in the winter keep them at around 16°C (61°F). When the parent plant dies down wait until the offsets are a good size, 8–10 cm (3–4 in) long, cut them off, and root them in sand and peat in an 8 cm (3 in) pot, ideally in a warm place, in a propagator, or covered with a plastic bag.

The most easily found Bromeliads are:

Aechmea, with grey-green leaves patterned with silvery white. Most are flowering size, and the flower spike is silvery pink.

Billbergia, which has thinner leaves in clusters.

Cryptanthus, the small 'earth stars', flat and good for dish gardens.

Neoregelia, with strap-like leaves, sometimes red or purple at the centre.

Vriesia, with arching rosettes of striped or patterned leaves.

All these make long-lasting pot plants, particularly in a low place where their rosette shape and colours can be appreciated from above.

SPRING BULBS

It is not too late to put in bulbs for the house to flower in the winter. Six corms of crocus, for instance, put in a shallow pan or bowl in moist potting compost in a dark cupboard, will show shoots in January, and the delicate white Tazetta narcissi can be put in bowls, or in shallow dishes of pebbles and water. (See p. 77 for more suggestions.)

Cyclamen saved from last year and repotted in August or September will be leafing again, so keep them moist, the pots on saucers of damp gravel. And make sure that the bowls of bulbs you have already planted, now in their cool, dark place, are not dry.

AS PLANTS DIE DOWN

If it hasn't already happened in September, the leaves and stems of achimenes, sinningias and tuberous-rooted begonias will be yellowing and dying down now; if you want to keep them for next spring, put them in a cool place and let them dry out, twisting off the stems gently as soon as they come away easily and storing the pots on their sides until the spring when the tubers can be removed and started into growth again.

Annuals and Outdoor Plants

FOOD PLANTS AND FLOWERING PLANTS

Clear any window boxes or pots outside of all the plant debris left by the finished annuals if you haven't already done this. You could put in heathers, dwarf evergreens, sweet williams, forget-me-nots,

SOME PERMANENT PLANTS FOR WINDOW BOXES

DWARF CONIFERS

These little trees and shrubs need little attention and come into their own in winter when their colours really sing out. They can be permanent inhabitants of a window box, being joined by flowering bulbs in spring and flowering annuals in summer. They are so slow-growing that they are not likely to become an embarrassment as to height and girth.

These are all natural miniature trees and nothing to do with Bonsai, which are artificially miniatured full-size trees (and as such a little worrying – to me anyway). Some are prostrate (growing horizontally), some tall and thin, some bushy. They are called evergreen but they can be silver-grey, all tones of green, bronze, gold or yellow.

Some particularly good ones to look out for are:
Chamaecyparis obtusa 'Nana', a rich dark green;
C. pisifera 'Compacta', grey-green;
C. pisifera 'Plumosa Aurea Nana', golden yellow;
Juniperus communis 'Compressa', grey-blue;
J. virginiana 'Globosa', pale grey;
Picea mariana 'Nana', blue-grey, apple-green when young;
Thuja orientalis 'Rosedalis', purple-bronze in winter, golden green in spring, blue-green in summer;
T. occidentalis 'Rheingold' and *T. o. 'Hetz Pygmy'*, both golden yellow.

They can be planted, or set in a box still in their pots, at any time as they are quite hardy. They like a peat compost with a little added grit, and must not be allowed to get waterlogged or dry out.

HEATHERS

The heathers or heaths make good permanent window box plants too, as long as they have the right sort of acid soil (you can buy a special ericaceous compost mix). These are the callunas and the ericas, shrubby evergreen plants usually sold in flower in autumn and winter. They flower best in full sun and can be trimmed after flowering to keep them neat. They are all small – around 30 cm (1 ft). They can be planted (or set in a window box in their pots and packed round with peat) in spring or autumn.
Erica carnea flowers from January to March, with flowers of white, mauve, purple or pink.
Erica × darleyensis has pink, white and rose flowers from December to May.
Calluna vulgaris varieties (this is the wild heather or ling) have purple flowers from August to October, and the leaves turn orange in autumn.

wallflowers, polyanthus, primroses, lily-of-the-valley, pansies or spring bulbs instead.

Once you have done this you won't have to do anything to your outside boxes and pots until next spring, when you will start sowing annual seeds indoors for planting out later.

HERBS

Your perennial herbs – thyme, rosemary, sage, winter savory and chives – should all have a cool place to overwinter, and should then start putting on new leaf in spring. They will need some water, but very little, to keep their compost from drying out altogether, but if you have sown parsley and basil so as to have supplies through the winter, these will need more water, regular feeding, and as sunny and warm a spot as possible.

Plants to Buy

October, like September, is a good time to buy new plants, as they are not in strong growth and will have plenty of time to settle into their new environment, and it isn't yet too cold outside so you needn't worry about your new plants getting too cold on their way home. It is usually advisable to give any new plant a thorough watering in a bucket of water, leaving it there until bubbles have stopped rising to the surface, then draining it, before putting it in its place. Remember that even if plants like to be warm they should *not* be over radiators or too near fires, and they must never be in a draught. And, most important, they must get enough light even in winter.

Poinsettias, or, to call them by their proper name, *Euphorbia pulcherrima*, will be appearing in the shops around now, with their bright red bracts, or equally decorative cream or pink colours. For bright winter colour they are hard to beat. They last well in a reasonable temperature of 12–16°C (54–61°F) and in a bright light. It is difficult to manage the right conditions in the home to bring these plants through the year to flower again, so they are better treated as temporary. They like a lot of water, but let the compost dry out a bit before watering again as overwatering causes the leaves to drop.

You might also find solanum, the winter cherry, which lasts a long time if kept fairly cool and sprayed regularly.

The seed catalogues will begin to be sent out about now, so you will be able to start thinking about what you want to order for next year. You will make yourself popular with the seedsmen if you place your orders in really good time rather than leaving it to the very last minute.

WINTER TEMPERATURES

This seems a good time for brief notes on the winter temperatures of plants, as some of them will be going into the cooler positions they need for their dormant period. Those which have to be kept in a normal living room with its higher temperatures will need more water and more frequent spraying and will not really rest. Winter temperatures are important as there is less light and air than in summer, and in reasonably well-heated rooms the background warmth is much greater.

Naturally every room and every window is different, and there are many 'climates' in one room, but as a rough guide recommended central heating temperatures are:

Living rooms	18–21°C (64–70°F)
Bedrooms	12–16°C (54–61°F)
Halls and spare rooms	10–12°C (50–54°F)

For plants for which a winter minimum temperature of around 18°C (64°F) is recommended, a sill or table in an average living room should do. My living room with a stove usually maintains this temperature; it obviously drops a bit at night or when I am away, but not for long, and the plants seem to be quite happy. Do remember, though, that plants left on the window side of a curtain at night will be liable to get much colder.

The needs of individual plants are given in the Glossary (see p. 102); see also p. 61 on winter temperatures for ferns.

GUIDE TO TEMPERATURE DEFINITIONS

Warm By 'warm' I mean 18–24°C (64–75°F). 24°C (75°F) is really a hothouse temperature, needing damp greenhouse conditions to keep up humidity, but many plants will manage in warm living rooms, particularly if given extra humidity by means of standing pots on moist pebbles or gravel or in damp peat and frequent mist-spraying.

Normal room By 'normal room' temperatures I mean from 10°C (50°F), very cool (my hall, for example), to 21°C (70°F). Most plants, people, and furniture do best in 'temperate' conditions, between 13°C (55°F) and 20°C (68°F).

Cool By a 'cool' winter resting temperature I mean 5–15°C (41–59°F).

All these can go up or down a bit without dire consequences.

NOVEMBER

Poor November suffers from being generally thought of as a totally grey month, foggy and bleak. But there can be wonderful golden days, with perhaps the last of the leaves falling from the trees. There is the smell of bonfires and fireworks, the rustle of dead leaves, electric lights reflected in damp pavements, fireside teas and muffins, and the warmth of rooms on dark evenings. Nevertheless there may well be fogs, windows will more and more often need to be shut, the days are getting ever shorter and the outlook will often be grey and depressing.

Luckily there are many flowering plants to cheer us up in the winter – cyclamen, capsicums, solanums, flowering cacti and primulas among them. The little *Begonia semperflorens* will still be flowering, and if you are one of those people for whom African violets perform, then you will have those. Anybody can grow impatiens, busy lizzie, and they will be in flower now too. The bowls of spring bulbs you put in in August or September may be beginning to show pale shoots, and the seed catalogues will be about, full of ideas for plants to grow from seed or buy as seedlings next year.

All the plants in the house should be well settled in their winter quarters by now, those brought nearer the windows now it is cooler looking clean and glossy in the autumn sun, but they will still need attention. Apart from keeping their compost moist, it is extremely important to keep up humidity around them and keep their leaves clean and shining.

November

TO BUY

PLANTS FOR CHRISTMAS NOW IN SHOPS, INCLUDING CAPSICUMS, CHRISTMAS CACTUS, CHRYSANTHEMUMS, CYCLAMEN, POINSETTIAS, PRIMULAS AND SOLANUMS

SEED CATALOGUES IN CIRCULATION

IN FLOWER

CINERARIA, CYCLAMEN, PRIMULAS AND SCHLUMBERGERA STARTING TO FLOWER

APHELANDRA SQUARROSA AND POINSETTIA STILL FLOWERING – AND OF COURSE THE YEAR-ROUND PLANTS LIKE *BEGONIA SEMPERFLORENS*, CHRYSANTHEMUM, *EUPHORBIA MILII*, IMPATIENS AND SAINTPAULIA

CANE-STEMMED BEGONIAS PROBABLY FINISHING, AND LAST GERANIUMS

ARDISIA, CAPSICUMS AND SOLANUM FRUITING

OUTSIDE ONLY ERICA HEATHERS FLOWERING

1 Schefflera actinophylla
2 Hedera helix
3 Chamaedorea elegans
4 Ficus pumila
5 Adiantum
6 Asplenium nidus
7 Pellaea rotundifolia
8 Epiphyllum
9 Crassula argentea
10 Astrophytum
11 Opuntia
12 Echeveria
13 Haworthia
14 Chamaecereus
15 Kalanchoe blossfeldiana

Looking After Your Houseplants

WATERING, FEEDING

Very important . . . under-, rather than overwater. Most plants are resting or at any rate running very slow, and just need to be kept slightly moist, though those in warm rooms will need more water. The exceptions are, of course, those plants that are putting on growth and coming into flower now, like the Christmas cactus and cyclamen, and these are also the only plants you should be feeding. Then there is cyperus, which likes to stand with its pot in a bowl of water all the time; it is only too easy to forget how quickly this dries up in a warm room.

HUMIDITY

Though most of the plants will need much less water than in the summer, those that are in warm, dry rooms will probably need just as much spraying to keep up the humidity around them. Remember that water for plants should always be at room temperature – which means tepid in a warm winter room – as this is less of a shock to the plants than cold water would be.

It makes it easier to keep up the humidity round plants if several are grouped together on a tray lined with moist peat or pebbles and sprayed frequently. They will combine to make their own micro-climate, arums and palms above, rex begonias and peperomias below. Chamaedorea, the parlour palm, is a great favourite of mine. It always looks good, and does well even in dryish rooms, given the occasional spray, quietly producing new spears of leaves all through the year. Other plants that look good in groups, particularly if they can be viewed from above, are the rosette-forming bromeliads.

Apart from the bathroom the good old kitchen window sill is a good place for ailing plants as they are under your eye a lot of the time and can be sprayed easily. And even a short stay in a cool place like a spare room or bathroom will be a tonic to plants suffering in a stuffy, dry atmosphere.

POSITION

As has already been said, the plants should all be well settled in their winter positions by now. Remember that plants should always be kept away from the direct heat of fires and radiators, and out of draughts – they hate draughts. Remember also that the space between window and curtains on a sill can be very cold on a frosty night, and that any plants there might be safer on a table near the window.

KEEPING THE LEAVES CLEAN

All through the winter it is important to see that the resting plants, which may well be somewhere you do not necessarily go every day, are kept free of dust and spiders' webs, poor things. I sometimes see dusty, sad plants in houses in winter, and long to give them a wash and an airing, and put them in the bathroom or kitchen where they will get some attention. Wiping the leaves and spraying with tepid water will freshen up any plant.

SPRING BULBS

If the bowls of spring bulbs you put in in August or September are beginning to show pale shoots, they can be moved out of the cold cupboard into a low light, where the temperature should be 16–18°C (61–64°F). When the leaves are well developed, and flower buds are beginning to show, they can go into a bright place where they can be admired. Don't worry too much if you did not plant any though, as there are plenty around in the shops for Christmas.

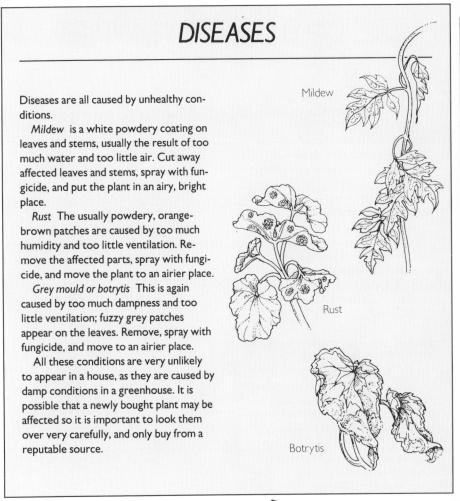

DISEASES

Diseases are all caused by unhealthy conditions.

Mildew is a white powdery coating on leaves and stems, usually the result of too much water and too little air. Cut away affected leaves and stems, spray with fungicide, and put the plant in an airy, bright place.

Rust The usually powdery, orange-brown patches are caused by too much humidity and too little ventilation. Remove the affected parts, spray with fungicide, and move the plant to an airier place.

Grey mould or botrytis This is again caused by too much dampness and too little ventilation; fuzzy grey patches appear on the leaves. Remove, spray with fungicide, and move to an airier place.

All these conditions are very unlikely to appear in a house, as they are caused by damp conditions in a greenhouse. It is possible that a newly bought plant may be affected so it is important to look them over very carefully, and only buy from a reputable source.

Mildew

Rust

Botrytis

AS PLANTS DIE DOWN

That pretty *Campanula isophylla* will finish flowering about now. When it does it should be cut hard back and rested, perhaps with the geraniums, with very little water, over the winter.

PROPAGATION TIPS

Seeds
Catalogues should be about now for next year.

Cuttings
Can take leaf cuttings or certain stem cuttings that are easy to root.

Bulbs
Plant hippeastrum for Christmas flowering.

BOTTLE GARDENS AND OTHER TERRARIUMS

This sort of enclosed gardening began quite accidentally 150 years ago when an English doctor, Nathaniel Ward, put a moth chrysalis in a small quantity of garden soil in a test tube in his laboratory and sealed it. Dr Ward wanted to study the moth emerging but was interested to see that a small fern started to grow in this sealed container, and even more interested to see that instead of dying for lack of air and water it grew and flourished. He then experimented with other seeds and plants, and came to the conclusion that tropical foliage plants, difficult to keep well and happy in a Victorian interior, seemed to do very well enclosed in their own humid atmosphere in a glass box. These miniature glass houses not only became very popular and fashionable in the smart interiors of the time, but were also used to transport rare plants by sea from their homes in the tropics to Europe, thus ensuring that many more of them survived the voyage.

The original Wardian cases, bottle gardens and fern cases are all closed plant cases. The plants in these boxes are self-supporting as water in the compost is taken up by the plants and given off into the surrounding atmosphere by the leaves, condensing on the glass and running back into the soil. The enclosed plants, like those in an open environment, take in oxygen at night and give off carbon dioxide in the daytime, and in this well-balanced micro-climate should need very little attention. Dr Ward claimed that one of his cases was completely undisturbed and healthy for 15 years.

WHAT TO USE

Any glass container can be used as long as it is made of clear glass; coloured glass will not let in enough light. Bell jars and glass sweet jars with stoppers may be used for single plants such as small ferns and selaginellas, and plants in a shallow container covered with a bell jar or Victorian glass dome will be as decorative as wax flowers with the added interest of being real. As designers and plantsmen are recognizing the decorative value of the traditional Victorian designs, more are becoming available and they are well worth looking for.

Ready-made boxes can be bought in both glass and plastic, ranging in size from small boxes for a single tiny plant to those large enough to hold a small indoor jungle. They all have fitted lids, most have adjustable air vents, and there are very sophisticated versions with heating and lighting equipment.

A 450 g (1 lb) jam jar with a lid can be a home for a single fern or African violet.

COMPOST

When planting one of these cases you must make sure that it is absolutely clean. The small jungle must have good drainage,

so a layer of gravel 3–6 mm (⅛–¼ in) in diameter – pea gravel – should go in first, 2.5 cm (1 in) deep in a small case and double that in a large one. On top of this goes a 5–8 cm (2–3 in) layer of peat compost. A teaspoon or two of powdered charcoal should be added to the gravel or compost to keep it sweet. In the case of narrow-necked containers such as carboys or bottles the compost will have to be poured in through a cardboard tube, and given a shake to level it.

TOOLS

Some garden shops sell special tools for bottle gardening, but you can make long-handled small forks and trowels by wiring old forks and spoons to bamboo canes, to manipulate the plants. A cotton reel or cork on the end of a cane will be useful for firming down the compost after planting.

WHAT TO PLANT

Naturally the plants you choose must be small to start with. Large terrariums, 70 cm (28 in) high, 55 cm (22 in) long, and 20 cm (8 in) wide, will hold three large and two small plants. Avoid quick growers as they will soon take over and swamp the slower ones. Flowering plants are better left out unless you can get to them easily, as dead flowers must be constantly removed as they can start all sorts of trouble with mould and fungus.

Obviously a group of plants sharing a case must all need and enjoy basically the same conditions, and, above all, they must be moisture-loving. The last plants to consider here are the dry-situation plants like cacti and succulents.

Ideal plants are all varieties of fittonia, small peperomias, adiantum (maidenhair ferns), sonerila, small ivies, small palms, and maranta, the prayer plant, notoriously difficult in rooms. Trailing plants like scindapsus are happy, too, in larger cases. For small cases and bottles pellaea ferns, selaginella, and *Peperomia caperata* are a good choice, and for larger ones maranta, *Calathea lancifolia* and *C. ornata*, the chamaedorea palm, *Dracaena sanderiana*, and ivies are ideal. Most hardy ferns found in the wild will take to a fern case: *Phyllitis scolopendrium* (hart's tongue), the wall ferns *Asplenium adiantum-nigrum* and *A. lanceolatum*, and small plants of blechnum and polystychum will all do well, and in larger cases *Pteris cretica*, the ribbon fern.

HOW TO PLANT

Take the plants out of their pots, make a small hole in the compost, and drop them in, easing the compost over the roots with your cork or fork and gently firming it down. When all the plants are in place you can wipe off any smears on the inside of the glass with cotton wool on the end of a cane. The box-type terrarium is of course easier to plant.

HOW TO LOOK AFTER THEM

In completely closed cases condensation may cloud the glass, and when this happens the lid must be opened slightly to ventilate it. Plants in a terrarium with a small opening, such as a bottle garden, will need watering occasionally, perhaps once a month, but nothing like as much as if they were in the open atmosphere of a room. Those in completely closed cases should need none at all.

You could give the plants an occasional feed, but less than plants growing ordinarily as you do not want them to get too large.

All these cases need to be in a good light but out of direct sun, so a north- or east-facing window is ideal. The temperature should be 20–22°C (68–72°F).

Dead leaves must be removed as they fall, and after a year or two you will either have to prune the larger plants or remove them to a pot of their own and replace them. The suppliers of the cases will be able to give you any more information you need.

Plants to Buy

SOLANUM

Pot plants to decorate the house for Christmas are now in the shops. One of the most common is of course poinsettia, and another is solanum, the winter or Jerusalem cherry, with its shiny red, yellow and white fruits ripening from green. It will keep its berries for months if it is kept well watered and sprayed every day for humidity. For all flowering or fruiting plants indoors dryness is the enemy, particularly if the room is warm. Keep it in a coolish place, 8–10°C (46–50°F) if possible. Be very fierce with children if you have one of these plants: it is a relative of the deadly nightshade as well as of the potato, and the berries are poisonous. This is usually treated as a disposable plant, and discarded when the fruits are over, unless you have room to cut it hard back, repot in rich soil, put it somewhere outside for the summer, and keep it to bring indoors again to fruit next autumn.

CAPSICUMS

Also of the potato family, the decorative capsicums or peppers make good colourful houseplants for the winter. They are bushy little plants with red, green and yellow cone-shaped fruits; they are annuals and discarded when the leaves shrivel. They like a good bright position.

CHRISTMAS CACTUS

Traditional for Christmas, as it flowers in winter, is *Schlumbergera truncata*, the Christmas cactus, also called zygocactus, and sometimes by its old name of epiphyllum to complicate matters still further. It is an epiphyte (like the bromeliads perching on the branches of forest trees) from the Brazilian tropics, with red or purple trumpet-shaped flowers at the end of its flat, leaf-like stems. Put it in a light place out of direct sunlight, and try not to let the temperature go below 12°C (54°F) or above 16°C (61°F). When the flower buds start to form in autumn it needs a lot of water, and feeding once a week. Its care and behaviour are thus completely opposite to that of most plants, as its resting period is in the summer, when the soil should be kept dry and the plant should be in as cool a place as possible. Sections of stem root well if taken in the summer. The flowering period should last from November to January, and all this time the compost should be kept moist and the humidity kept up by daily spraying.

CYCLAMEN

Probably the favourite pot plants for presents are cyclamen, which appear in the shops in November. They are very pretty with heart-shaped, often marbled leaves and shuttlecock-shaped flowers, and they go on flowering through the winter if kept in a cool place (10–16°C/50–61°F). A north-facing window sill suits them well as, like most flowering plants, they will droop in the sun. The compost should be kept just moist while the plant is flowering, and at the end of the winter when it begins to die down less and less water should be given so as to allow it to dry out. Yellow leaves and dead flowers should be pulled off gently and the corm kept quite dry in summer if you want to keep it for another season. Store it in a cool place, indoors or outside on a shady balcony or sill. The corm is then repotted in new compost in August, and when leaves appear it should be given a feed every 2 weeks. Cyclamen like soft water, and this should be kept off the corms; it suits them to stand on a tray or bowl of wet pebbles. Plants with a lot of flower and leaf are thirsty souls and may need watering twice a day.

CINERARIA

Cineraria appear in the shops now with their clusters of bright daisy flowers, red, pink, purple or white. Like chrysanthemums, which are also in the shops in abundance at this time of year, they are disposable. Give them a cool place out of direct sunlight, generous quantities of water, and fresh air when possible.

DECEMBER

December means Christmas, cosiness, fires, decorations, presents. With parties in the offing, do make sure your plants are all right, as dreadful things can happen to them at parties: cigarette ash and cigarette ends, even unwanted drinks, are tipped into flower pots, plants are knocked into, and tender leaves get damaged. So put your poor plants in safe corners well out of the way – and out of draughts, too.

The other great event is the winter solstice, the shortest day. A great moment in the year this, particularly for gardeners, when – magic time – the days start getting longer, almost imperceptibly at first, and the evenings lighter.

Many houseplants change hands as presents over Christmas, and they should all be looking their best at this time with shiny clean leaves. Splashes of colour will come from the poinsettias, solanums and azaleas as well as from your holly berries, and you might have some early daffodils, crocuses or hyacinths to remind you that spring is not far away. The Christmas cactus, with its bright crimson or purple flowers, will look best hanging down from a high spot, while pots of pink and white cyclamen on saucers of damp pebbles will look pretty on tables and sills.

Even for people with gardens this is a quiet time of year and an ideal one for perusing the seed catalogues and making plans and dreaming dreams about next year. But don't forget the houseplants while you dream your dreams. You will need to keep an eye on them constantly to make sure they are all right.

DECEMBER

TO BUY

FLOWERING PLANTS SUCH AS AZALEAS, CAPSICUMS, CINERARIA, CYCLAMEN, POINSETTIA, PRIMULAS, AND SOLANUM, BOTH TO DECORATE THE HOUSE AND AS PRESENTS

NORFOLK ISLAND PINE, A POSSIBLE ALTERNATIVE CHRISTMAS TREE

ORDER SEEDS AND SEEDLINGS FOR NEXT SPRING

IN FLOWER

AZALEA, COELOGYNE, JASMINE, KALANCHOE, AND PAPHIOPEDILUM STARTING TO FLOWER

THE EARLIEST SPRING BULBS MIGHT BE STARTING

APHELANDRA SQUARROSA, CYCLAMEN, POINSETTIA, PRIMULAS AND SCHLUMBERGERA STILL FLOWERING

CAPSICUMS AND SOLANUM FRUITING

OUTSIDE: ERICA HEATHERS FLOWERING

1	Jasminum polyanthum
2	Euphorbia pulcherrima
3	Schlumbergera 'Bridgesii'
4	Cyclamen persicum
5	Araucaria
6	Rhododendron simsii
7	Maranta
8	Euphorbia splendens

Looking After Your Houseplants

WATERING, FEEDING, HUMIDITY

In the bleak midwinter you must watch the houseplants for yellowing and dropping leaves. This can be due to either over- or underwatering. The state of the compost will tell you which; the most usual cause is too much water. As we have already noticed, resting plants need much less water than when they are in full growth — and no food at all. You will need to keep up regular spraying, however, and on mild days open a window to give your plants some fresh air from time to time.

Look at the wintering geraniums and cacti and succulents often to see that they are all right. Remove dead leaves and keep the compost barely moist.

POSITION

If you do give your plants some fresh air on mild days, be sure they do not get chilled or put in a draught. On frosty nights never leave them on the window side of curtains.

KEEPING THE LEAVES CLEAN

Keep an eye on all the plants, particularly those with shiny, leathery leaves, and make sure they are free of dust — regular spraying and wiping will keep them healthy. Palms especially benefit from having their leaves kept clean.

SPRING BULBS

Some of the earliest bulbs will be showing flower buds this month, and should be put into a brighter light. Remember to keep their compost always moist.

Plants to Buy

In December you will probably find yourself buying plants both to cheer up the house and to give away as presents – a plant always makes an acceptable gift. There are lots of houseplants, foliage ones and flowering ones, to choose from. Only take care you don't let them get too cold on your way back from the shop.

NORFOLK ISLAND PINE

There is a lovely indoor 'tree' which is particularly appropriate at Christmas time, as it is a branched pine tree, growing to 60 m (200 ft) in its homeland, the Norfolk Islands in the South Pacific. The Norfolk Island pine is an araucaria, which makes it a cousin of the monkey puzzle tree. It has horizontal tiers of foliage, rather like fossilized fern leaves, and is an ideal houseplant as it seldom grows to more than 1.5 m (5 ft) indoors and is slow-growing. It is suitable for halls and staircases as it likes a cool place. In its home it is used as a Christmas tree, and it could well be here too as long as its branches are not overladen with decorations. The araucaria would be happy in a north light, and needs a certain amount of moisture; it must be kept out of the sun in summer, and the winter temperature should not go below 5°C (41°F). A peat- or loam-based compost will suit it, and young plants should be potted on every year until they are in a 20–25 cm (8–10 in) pot. You should be able to find them in the shops all the year round.

PRIMULAS

Flowering plants are naturally popular in the middle of winter and primulas come into flower now – or even in November; there are two easily available in the shops, *Primula malacoides* and *P. obconica*.

HUMIDITY

Keeping up the correct level of humidity round certain plants makes an enormous difference to their general health and growth. Many ferns such as adiantum will grow quite reasonably without it, but will improve out of all recognition given the right amount. We all know that the dry atmosphere of central heating can be bad for human beings and old furniture; it can be nearly fatal for plants.

It is important to mist-spray most plants in the dry days of summer, and perhaps even more so in the dry heated rooms of winter. 40–60 per cent moisture in the air is generally regarded as right for living rooms; in the rain forests philodendrons live in 60–100 per cent, whereas in the deserts succulents revel in 10 per cent. Centrally heated rooms can drop to desert dryness. Failing a humidifier you can improve conditions by placing bowls of water round the room. Plants that overwinter in very cold positions will not need spraying, or hardly at all.

WAYS OF KEEPING UP HUMIDITY

Mist-spraying daily is an excellent refresher for most plants (but not the hairy or furry-leaved ones). Stand far enough away from the plant to allow the spray to be a mist and not a rainstorm of drops, avoid the furniture as much as possible, and never spray in bright sunlight.
Double pot method Another way of keeping up humidity is to use the double pot method: stand the plant pot in a larger container packed round with damp peat.
Using moist pebbles A third way is to put the pots on trays or dishes filled with pebbles or gravel and water, the base of the pot on the pebbles not in the water.

Groups of plants on trays or in containers of peat will benefit more than individual ones as more humidity will be conserved by all the plants together.

The humidity levels for individual plants are given in the Glossary (see p. 102).

GUIDE TO HUMIDITY TERMS

High Plants requiring a high level of humidity will need to be mist-sprayed frequently, probably daily, or to be stood on moist pebbles or in damp peat. If you stand pots on pebbles or in peat you will usually not have to spray plants so often. Some plants require an exceptionally high degree of humidity, however, often plants that would really be better off in a greenhouse, enclosed plant window, or terrarium, and these should be sprayed daily and placed on moist pebbles or in damp peat.
Average Most plants do not need to be stood on moist pebbles or in damp peat but would nevertheless do that little bit better if they were. A mist-spray every week or so (or more if in a very warm room) would probably be just as good, but you may not remember to do it. Standing pots on pebbles or in peat is an easy way of ensuring that plants are happy without you having to remember to spray so often. Only plants that need more than average humidity *need* this, but many more will *enjoy* it.
Low For plants that like a low level of humidity an occasional mist-spray just to freshen them up is all they need.
None Cacti and succulents (except forest cacti) thrive in a very dry atmosphere and do not like any humidity around them at all. Avoid spraying them and do not put them in rooms like bathrooms and kitchens with a naturally humid atmosphere.

PROPAGATION TIPS

Seeds
Remember to order seeds for next year.

Cuttings
Can take leaf cuttings and stem cuttings of particularly easy plants.

P. malacoides came from China at the beginning of the century and immediately became a great favourite; it has delicate, scented flowers which go on for weeks, dark pink, pale mauve or white, and providing you remove dead flowers regularly it will continue to look springlike for 2–3 months. The plants must be kept moist and need a fresh, well-ventilated place; regular spraying will keep up the humidity they need. A good light is desirable but not too much heat; the temperature should not rise above 16°C (61°F), and 12°C (54°F) is ideal.

P. obconica has larger flowers, rather like primroses, in large clusters, and needs the same treatment and care. The long-lasting flowers (dead-head assiduously) are red, pink or mauve and all colours in between. The drawback to this pretty plant is that the small hairs on the stem can cause extreme irritation to people allergic to such things. Both these primulas, like most flowering plants, will have more flowers over a longer period if they are in a cool room rather than a warm one.

Cyclamen, as mentioned before (see p. 94), will also last much longer in a cool place, around 10–16°C (50–61°F).

AZALEAS

These are popular as presents and very thirsty customers indeed. It is difficult to overwater azaleas, particularly in a warm room, and they must have humidity or all the flowers and buds will drop off. Bowls of bulbs make good presents too, as do the primulas in pots, and of course cyclamen.

PLASTIC PLANTS

There are some places where a plant is called for where even the most tolerant could not survive, or where you would have to get a stepladder to water it. There is a very good case to be made for plastic plants in this situation – an amazing

LIGHT REQUIREMENTS OF PLANTS

As with all other aspects of plant care, different plants have very different likes and dislikes as regards light and position. While cacti, succulents and geraniums and some other sun-lovers like to spend the summer months basking in the hottest sun, other plants are quite happy on a sunny sill in winter but should be kept out of the sun in summer, others like a bright light but should always be kept out of direct sun, and yet others positively like some degree of shade. Some of the more tolerant plants will perhaps do best in a good bright light but will be all right in a darker position. Most, but not all, flowering plants are better out of direct sunlight. The light requirements for individual plants are given in the Glossary (see p. 102).

GUIDE TO DEFINITIONS OF LIGHT REQUIREMENTS

Bright and sunny Self-explanatory; a south-facing window sill or porch is ideal.
Shaded from the hottest sun Do not put in a south window or porch unless shaded by another plant or some way back from the window. An east or west window would be ideal, or a table a little way back from a south window.
Bright light out of direct sun A good bright place facing north or east (as the early morning sun is not too hot), or a table near a window where the rays of the sun do not strike the plant directly.
Semi-shade In the dappled shade of another plant, in the shade of a very thin curtain or venetian blind, or a little further back in the room, but not as far away from direct sunlight as 'shade'.
Shade Some way back from a window, or completely shaded by another plant.
Low A good way from a window, possibly in a fairly dark place like a hall.

PALMS

If you asked a number of people to name the indoor plant with the most style most of them would probably say palms. They were for a time quite out of fashion as they were associated, to their detriment, with Victorian plush and Edwardian palm court orchestras, but they are now as popular as ever – and rightly so as, apart from their grace, they are very easy-going houseplants and quite tough customers.

The howeas, also called kentias, are not very thirsty plants, but as they do not have a complete rest in the winter but continue slowly to send up their spear-like sheaths of new leaves, they need a little more water in winter than most plants. They never like a lot of water, just a little less in winter than in summer.

Palms are easy to place in rooms, as, coming from shady places, they do not have to be near a window. They like soft water or rain water – hard water tends to make the leaf tips go brown. A normal room temperature suits them; they can even live in 27°C (80°F), but it should never go below 12°C (54°F).

One of my absolute favourites is the parlour palm, *Chamaedorea elegans*, which

ARTIFICIAL LIGHT AND PLANTS

It is sometimes necessary to supplement natural light with artificial light. Fine specimen plants such as palms and dracaenas can be illuminated by spotlights which give dramatic shadows and decorative focus, and these give marginal extra light to the plants.

The real daylight substitute is given by fluorescent tubes; Cool White and Daylight 40 watt tubes are ideal. These should be in groups of two and 45–75 cm (18–30 in) above the plants to really affect their growth in a darkish place. There should be a screen or shade to keep them from shining in people's eyes and to concentrate light on the plants. Alcoves, niches and shelf units all lend themselves to plant displays lit by fluorescent tubes. Plants which seem to do especially well growing under artificial light are African violets.

comes from Mexico. It is a small palm, and slow-growing, needing less water than its relations, and is happy quite some distance away from a light source. *Chamaerops humilis* is the only indigenous European palm, growing round the Mediterranean; it has leaves like Chinese fans on long stems. The date palm, which can be grown from a stone, if you are lucky, is *Phoenix dactylifera*, and this is a fast grower for a palm. It is easy-going and can survive low temperatures. Two of its more dwarf relations make lovely houseplants – *P. canariensis* and *P. roebelinii*.

suggestion from someone who is dotty about plants. The long gallery at Chenenceau, that most magical of Loire chateaux, has magnificent plants in every niche, looking tremendous . . . they are plastic.

LOOKING AHEAD

Do get hold of the seed catalogues if you have not already done so, and look at the various plants which can be raised from seed in the house such as tomatoes, aubergines and peppers, ipomoea (morning glory), geraniums, and many of the tropical houseplants; also the useful sprouting seeds, which can be grown any time. And don't forget that you must order early if you want small seedlings of the special small-scale tomatoes and other fruiting plants to pot on when you receive them in May, thus avoiding the hassle of seed-sowing.

Glossary

SCOPE OF THE GLOSSARY

The Glossary covers only houseplants proper – those mentioned in the main text of this book and the more common ones you are likely to come across in nurseries and shops. It does not, however, cover food plants, herbs, flowering annuals, spring bulbs, or dwarf conifers and heathers, although all these feature in the text. This is partly for reasons of space, but mainly because it would be unnecessarily cumbersome to include them: the requirements, in terms of care, of one herb and another, or of one dwarf conifer and another, are so similar that it would be pointless to set them out separately for each plant. All these are dealt with in boxes in the main part of the book, however, as well as in the text itself.

PURPOSE OF THE GLOSSARY

The Glossary is intended as a complete reference section. A brief description and line drawing of each plant should enable you to identify it, and a rough indication of size is also given for each plant: you will not, for example, want to buy a musa (the banana palm), which can grow to 3 m (10 ft), if what you actually want is a plant for a little table by a window.

The Glossary also gives detailed instructions on the care of each plant, under the following headings:

Compost This tells you what type of compost each plant prefers. The whole subject of compost, and special compost mixes, is dealt with in detail on pp. 17 and 20.

Temperature This tells you how warm or cold each plant likes to be, in summer and winter. Do remember, however, that plants are on the whole very tolerant. The temperatures given here are the ideal ones, and a bit cooler or a bit warmer usually won't do any harm, though you may need to give less water if a plant is in a cool place and more water and more mist-sprays if it is in a very warm room. For a rough guide to the terms 'warm', 'normal room' and 'cool', as used in the Glossary, see p. 86.

Light Once again plants are mostly very tolerant, but this does tell you where a plant will be likely to do best. If you are looking for a plant for a particular position – for example, a south-facing window – it will obviously make sense to buy a plant that you know will thrive in those conditions. Explanations of the terms used in the Glossary are given on p. 100.

Watering A very subjective matter this – as I have already said, what seems almost dry to one person seems wringing wet to another – but it is nevertheless true that more plants suffer from overwatering than from anything else. Because of different conditions it is impossible to say exactly how often plants should be watered and how much. What you need to do is to get to know when your individual plants need water. The Glossary can give you a rough idea of the requirements of each plant. See p. 26 for more information on watering.

Humidity Providing adequate humidity is often just as important as watering, and requirements do vary enormously. While cacti and succulents mostly like to be bone dry, ferns like a very moist atmosphere; and most plants will need spraying in warm, dry, centrally heated rooms and on hot summer days. See p. 99 for different methods of providing humidity.

Feeding Most plants need to be fed for some part of the year. The Glossary tells you when and how often. For more information on feeding, see p. 28.

Propagation Some plants are very easy to propagate, some extremely difficult. The Glossary tells you the method(s) which will be most likely to succeed with each plant. All the different methods are dealt with in detail on pp. 70–71, except for taking whole leaf cuttings, which is on p. 10.

Flowering season This is given where applicable – though obviously in practice plants may flower a bit earlier or a bit later, depending on circumstances.

One last word: the Glossary is meant to help you care for your plants properly, not to make you constantly anxious that you might not be catering adequately for their every need. I have said repeatedly but will say again that plants are for the most part extremely tolerant: the information in the Glossary should be taken as a rough guide and never as hard-and-fast rules.

ABUTILON · *Malvaceae* · Flowering Maple

Easily grown evergreen shrub, with maple-shaped leaves, sometimes variegated. Orange, yellow or purple flowers are produced in the summer. The plants can be cut back rigorously as they speedily shoot again, and the cuttings root easily. Grows to 1.2 m (4 ft).

COMPOST Loam-based.
TEMPERATURE Normal room; 12–15°C (54–59°F) autumn and winter.
LIGHT A bright light by a window, in or out of the sun.
WATER Plenty in summer, sometimes twice a day; very little in winter.
HUMIDITY Moderate; spray occasionally.
FEEDING Weekly April–October.
PROPAGATION From tip cuttings in summer.
FLOWERING SEASON May–September.

ACHIMENES · *Gesneriaceae* · Hot Water Plant

A hothouse plant, or temporary houseplant, needing humidity, with tubular, trumpet-shaped flowers, red, purple, pink or white, in summer and early autumn. It grows from rhizomes in the early spring, which are planted four to six in a 10 cm (4 in) pot, or six to eight in a 15 cm (6 in) one. It can be dried off in the winter, stored, and started into growth again any time from January to March. When stems have died down cut them off and store pots on their sides. Up to 60 cm (2 ft). (See also p. 11.)

COMPOST Peat-based.
TEMPERATURE Normal room (around 16°C/61°F) while growing, cool (around 7°C/45°F) while dried off in winter.
LIGHT Bright, by a window, but out of direct sunlight.
WATER After potting water sparingly; while growth is strong, give more. Give less gradually as flowers die off, and none at all while plants are dried off for the winter. Use tepid water.
HUMIDITY High; spray frequently and stand on moist pebbles.
FEEDING Every 2 weeks from June to September.
PROPAGATION New rhizomes are produced each year, and can be separated, potted, and started into growth at 16–21°C (61–70°F).
FLOWERING SEASON June–September.

ADIANTUM · *Polypodiaceae* · Maidenhair Fern

Fern with delicate leaves and black wiry stems. *A. capillus veneris* is the common maidenhair fern; with its particularly delicate light green fronds it is the most popular of all the ferns. Height 15–40 cm (6–16 in).

COMPOST Well-drained peat-based mix.
TEMPERATURE Warm in summer, 16°C (61°F) in winter.
LIGHT Out of direct sunlight, in a draught-free, bright place.
WATER Water generously with tepid, soft water.
HUMIDITY High. Stand plants on moist pebbles in bowls or in a double pot packed round with moist peat. Spray daily with a fine mist-spray.
FEEDING Every 2 weeks May–August.
PROPAGATION By division of the roots in spring.

AECHMEA · *Bromeliaceae* · Urn Plant

A star-shaped rosette of grey-green, arched, sword-shaped leaves, up to 60 cm (2 ft) long, forming a funnel in the centre from which grows a silver-pink flowering stem.

COMPOST Peat.
TEMPERATURE Warm (16–24°C/61–75°F); will tolerate as low as 7°C (45°F) in winter, but 16°C (61°F) is better.
LIGHT Bright, without direct sun.
WATER Moderately in summer, with some in the central 'cup'; only enough to keep the soil barely moist in winter.
HUMIDITY Moderate, spray occasionally.
FEEDING Weak feed monthly, March–September.
PROPAGATION From offsets which form round the parent plant when the flower stem begins to die down.
FLOWERING SEASON Can produce flowers at any time of year, and dies after flowering.

AGAVE · *Agavaceae* · Century Plant

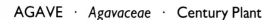

Agaves are slow-growing succulents, with rosettes of sword-shaped leaves. The narrow leaves are toothed, green, or, in *A. americana* 'Marginata', edged with yellow. They grow up to 30–38 cm (12–15 in) high in a pot.

COMPOST Loam-based, with sharp sand or grit added.
TEMPERATURE Very warm in summer, cool in winter (4–6°C/39–43°F).
LIGHT The best; a sunny sill is ideal.
WATER Keep on the dry side; water moderately in summer, keep almost dry in winter.
HUMIDITY None; keep dry.
FEEDING Dilute liquid feed every 2–3 weeks May–July.
PROPAGATION From offsets in spring or summer.

AGLAONEMA · *Araceae* · Chinese Evergreen

Small herbaceous perennials with variegated leaves, often silvery patterned on green. Growing to about 30–45 cm (12–18 in).

COMPOST Loam-based.
TEMPERATURE Warm; not below 13°C (55°F).
LIGHT Semi-shade.
WATER Freely in spring and summer, sparingly in winter.
HUMIDITY High; spray frequently and stand pot on damp pebbles or in moist peat.
FEEDING Fortnightly in the growing season, April–August.
PROPAGATION By division of mature plants in March or April.

ALOE · *Liliaceae*

Decorative rosette-forming plants. Two are commonly sold: *A. arborescens*, which is tree-shaped with spiny succulent leaves, growing erect, and *A. variegata*, the partridge-breasted aloe, which has a corkscrew rosette of triangular leaves striped with white. They have orange flowers borne 30 cm (12 in) high in loose racemes in March and April. Up to 30 cm (1 ft).

COMPOST Loam, peat and sharp sand.
TEMPERATURE Very warm in summer, cool in winter, 4–6°C (39–43°F).
LIGHT A good bright light, in sun.
WATER Generously in summer, sparingly in winter.
HUMIDITY None; keep dry.
FEEDING Every 2–3 weeks March–September.
PROPAGATION In spring or summer, from offsets, which root easily.
FLOWERING SEASON March and April.

APHELANDRA SQUARROSA · *Acanthaceae* · Zebra Plant

Decorative evergreen plants 30 cm (1 ft) tall and more, with glossy green leaves patterned and veined in white or yellow. Flower spikes are made up of closely overlapping yellow bracts, the flowers appearing in autumn and winter. It is usually bought flowering. Cut hard back after flowering and repot in spring.

COMPOST Rich, peat-based.
TEMPERATURE Warm throughout the year; not less than 12–16°C (54–61°F) in winter.
LIGHT Good, but out of direct sun.
WATER Generously in the growing and flowering period and more sparingly after flowering. Use soft water.
HUMIDITY High; spray frequently, and stand on damp pebbles or in moist peat.
FEEDING Fortnightly in the growing period.
PROPAGATION By cuttings from new shoots in spring.
FLOWERING SEASON October–January.

ARAUCARIA EXCELSA · *Araucariaceae* · Norfolk Island Pine

An evergreen coniferous tree with tiers of pine-needled leaves. It will reach over 60 m (200 ft) in the wild, but grows slowly in a pot up to about 1–1.5 m (3–5 ft). (See also p. 99.)

COMPOST Peat or loam.
TEMPERATURE Cool; in winter 5–10°C (41–50°F).
LIGHT Best in a north window; no direct sun.
WATER Moderate in summer, very little in winter.
HUMIDITY Likes moist air; spray every day or so in the growing season.
FEEDING Every 2 weeks March–September.
PROPAGATION From seed in spring.

ARDISIA CRISPA · *Myrsinaceae* · Coral Berry

A small evergreen shrub or small tree growing to about 60 cm (2 ft). It produces sweet-scented white flowers in late summer which later become decorative and long-lasting red berries.

COMPOST Loam-based.
TEMPERATURE Warm in summer (20–22°C/68–72°F), and 12–15°C (54–59°F) in winter, as the berries tend to drop if warmer.
LIGHT A good bright place, in sun in winter, but out of direct sunlight in summer.
WATER Moderate; keep just moist in winter.
HUMIDITY High; spray frequently with lukewarm water.
FEEDING Weekly May–September.
PROPAGATION From cuttings of lateral shoots in summer, or seed in spring.
FLOWERING SEASON Berries September–November. Flowers can appear at the same time, or a little earlier, for next year's berries.
NOTE The leaves sometimes produce nodules along the edges; these are harmless and should not be removed.

ARGYRODERMA · *Aizoaceae* · Mesems

Small, pebble-like succulent plants, with fat leaves that grow in pairs like split stones, and purple or yellow flowers in summer. Up to 5 cm (2 in) across.

COMPOST Loam, peat and sharp sand, or special cactus mix.
TEMPERATURE Very warm in summer, cool in winter.
LIGHT Bright and sunny.
WATER Sparingly in summer; keep almost dry in winter, giving the merest drop perhaps once a month.
HUMIDITY None; keep dry.
FEEDING Every 2–3 weeks May–September.
PROPAGATION From offsets or from seed, in spring or summer.
FLOWERING SEASON July and August.
NOTE Conophytum, faucaria and lithops are very similar plants, to be cared for in exactly the same way.

ASPARAGUS · *Liliaceae*

Ornamental rather than culinary asparagus. A. *setaceus* (syn. A. *plumosus*) is the well-known so-called 'fern' with delicate, feathery leaves – 'so-called' because it is not a fern, but a member of the lily family. Height 30 cm (12 in).

COMPOST Loam-based.
TEMPERATURE An even 12°C (54°F) throughout the year is ideal; it can survive temperatures as low as 5°C (41°F) for short periods.
LIGHT Good, but out of direct sun.
WATER Plenty from March to August; just keep moist in winter.
HUMIDITY High; spray leaves twice a day if in a dry situation, and stand on moist pebbles or in damp peat.
FEEDING Weekly in the growing season, April–September. Don't feed for 2 months after repotting.
PROPAGATION Divide the root clumps in March, potting up the outer portions.

ASPIDISTRA · *Liliaceae* · Cast Iron Plant

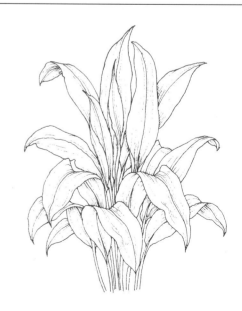

An old favourite with long, glossy, upright-growing, spear-shaped leaves, 30–45 cm (12–18 in) long. A very tolerant and easy plant.

COMPOST Loam- or peat-based.
TEMPERATURE Cool rather than warm, but tolerant.
LIGHT Prefers slight shade, but very adaptable. Can survive in quite dark places.
WATER Freely in summer, moderately in winter.
HUMIDITY Not essential as it will tolerate dry air, but it does better if sprayed frequently from March to August. Always keep the leaves wiped clean and free of dust.
FEEDING None generally. Very large established plants can have just two or three feeds between March and August.
PROPAGATION By root division in spring.

ASPLENIUM · *Aspleniaceae* · Spleenwort

This is a large genus of ferns; the most common as a houseplant is *A. nidus*, the bird's nest fern, with its glossy, vivid apple-green leaves growing out from a central point. It is an epiphyte, growing up to 1.2 m (4 ft). *A. adiantum-nigrum* and *A. lanceolatum* do well in an enclosed plant case.

COMPOST Quick-draining, peat-based.
TEMPERATURE Not below 16°C (61°F) in winter, otherwise easy.
LIGHT Fairly bright, but not in direct sun.
WATER Keep moist all the year round.
HUMIDITY Frequent mist-sprays in summer, and in winter if in a warm room. You could also stand pot on moist pebbles or in damp peat.
FEEDING Every 2 weeks March–September.
PROPAGATION Not worth trying.

AUCUBA JAPONICA · *Cornaceae*

Evergreen shrubs up to 2 m (7 ft) in height, with pointed glossy leaves, in some varieties flecked with yellow specks, and red berries in autumn and winter.

COMPOST Loam-based.
TEMPERATURE Cool; 4–6°C (39–43°F) minimum in winter, and ideally outside in summer, as it is a hardy plant.
LIGHT Low; a shady situation.
WATER Moderately in summer, very little in winter.
HUMIDITY Low; spray occasionally to keep plant fresh.
FEEDING Fortnightly April–August.
PROPAGATION By stem cuttings or from seed, in summer.

AZALEA · *Ericaceae*

These are usually called Indian azaleas (*A. indica*) and bought to flower as temporary houseplants; to flower next year, they have to be outdoors all the summer. Flowers are white, red, purple or pink. Height usually 30–60 cm (1–2 ft).

COMPOST Content for their flowering period in the compost they are bought in. Peat-based if you do keep them and repot.
TEMPERATURE Cool; ideally 12–16°C (54–61°F), and 4–6°C (39–43°F) minimum.
LIGHT Bright but out of direct sun.
WATER Use soft water (rain), and water freely. You can plunge the pots in a bucket of water every few days for 20 minutes instead of watering ordinarily.
HUMIDITY High; spray daily (try to avoid the flowers), and stand on trays of moist pebbles if possible.
FEEDING Every month from April, until flowering begins.
PROPAGATION Not possible at home.
FLOWERING SEASON December–February.

BEGONIA · *Begoniaceae* · Foliage Begonias and Flowering Begonias

The many varieties of *B. rex* make richly patterned and colourful foliage plants. The rhizomatous roots, the stems, and sometimes the undersides of the leaves are hairy. Grows up to 45 cm (18 in). (See also p. 53.)

COMPOST Loam or peat.
TEMPERATURE Around 15–20°C (59–68°F); not below 10°C (50°F).
LIGHT Good but out of direct sun; a north window is ideal.
WATER Water generously when the compost feels dry in summer; very little in winter.
HUMIDITY High in summer, and in winter if the air is dry; the double pot method is successful.
FEEDING Every 2 weeks April–September.
PROPAGATION Cuttings of sections of leaves can be rooted in warmth, in a propagator or under a plastic dome, at any time of year.

Flowering begonias may grow from tubers or fibrous roots.

The tuberous-rooted begonias are flowering plants for the summer, dying down in the winter; the tubers should be kept dry over the winter and started into growth again between January and March. 30–45 cm (12–18 in) high.

The fibrous-rooted semperflorens begonias live up to their name and flower most of the year; they are ideal for window boxes outside and also as houseplants. Stem cuttings root easily. Up to 30 cm (1 ft) tall.

Fibrous-rooted, shrubby or cane-stemmed begonias have the familiar asymmetrical 'angel's wing' leaves, grow to 1.2 m (4 ft) or more in a pot, and bear pink flowers from May to November.

COMPOST Loam or peat.
TEMPERATURE Moderate, not above 21°C (70°F); minimum 12°C (54°F).
LIGHT Bright, but not direct sun.
WATER Keep always moist.
HUMIDITY Moderate; spray occasionally, but do not let water fall on the flowers as they will mark.
FEEDING Every 2 weeks when growing fast; tomato fertilizer is good.
PROPAGATION 5–8 cm (2–3 in) stem cuttings root easily in peat and sand at 18°C (64°F) in summer. You can also take leaf cuttings of cane-stemmed and semperflorens begonias, using whole leaves.
FLOWERING SEASON June–September for tuberous-rooted begonias; May–November for cane-stemmed begonias, although they often go on flowering right through the winter; most of the year for *B. semperflorens*.

BELOPERONE GUTTATA · *Acanthaceae* · Shrimp Plant

Also known as drejerella, an easily grown and popular plant with soft green leaves and reddish brown bracts that resemble a shrimp's body. Height 30–60 cm (1–2 ft).

COMPOST Loam-based.
TEMPERATURE Normal room; in winter 12–16°C (54–61°F).
LIGHT Bright; out of direct sun in summer.
WATER Water freely in summer; keep just moist in winter.
HUMIDITY Average; spray occasionally.
FEEDING Every week March–September.
PROPAGATION Stem cuttings taken in spring or summer should root at 18°C (64°F).
FLOWERING SEASON Any time between April and November.

BILLBERGIA · *Bromeliaceae*

One of the 'indestructible' houseplants, it has long, pointed leaves in a rosette, with brilliant flower-like bracts. B. nutans is the most common; all are easy-going. 30–60 cm (1–2 ft) height and spread.

COMPOST Loam-based with added peat.
TEMPERATURE Ideally 16°C (61°F), but tolerant. Winter minimum 7°C (45°F).
LIGHT Bright, but out of direct sun.
WATER Freely in summer; keep just moist in winter.
HUMIDITY It can manage perfectly well without much humidity, but may do better if you stand it on moist pebbles.
FEEDING Monthly March–September.
PROPAGATION From offsets, 13–18 cm (5–7 in) high, in spring.
FLOWERING SEASON Mostly May–July.

BLECHNUM · *Polypodiaceae*

B. gibbum is one of the best and easiest of ferns for the house, growing to 1 m (3 ft) with light green glossy fronds.

COMPOST Peat-based.
TEMPERATURE Warm; not above 16–18°C (61–64°F) in winter.
LIGHT Shady, well-ventilated place.
WATER Generously in spring and summer, moderately in winter.
HUMIDITY High; spray frequently and stand pots on damp pebbles or in moist peat.
FEEDING Fortnightly in the growing season, April–August.
PROPAGATION By division of the roots in spring.

BROWALLIA · *Solanaceae*

Annual flowering shrubs 20–25 cm (8–10 in) high, which are relations of the nightshade and potato, usually bought in flower and then discarded. The long-lasting, star-shaped flowers are violet-blue with white centres, or white.

COMPOST Loam-based.
TEMPERATURE Normal room.
LIGHT Good, but out of direct sun.
WATER Generous.
HUMIDITY Spray occasionally.
FEEDING Weekly while flowering.
PROPAGATION From seed in spring, or in early autumn for winter flowering.
FLOWERING SEASON June–September, but B. speciosa major flowers in the winter.

BRUNFELSIA · *Solanaceae*

Shrubby plants growing to 1 m (3 ft), related to browallia, with cream or violet flowers between April and September; dormant from November to January. In winter they need little water after flowering stops.

COMPOST Peat-based.
TEMPERATURE Moderate when flowering, 13–20°C (55–68°F), and 12–14°C (54–57°F) in winter.
LIGHT Good, but out of direct sun.
WATER Generously in summer, little in winter.
HUMIDITY High; spray daily. It would also appreciate standing on moist pebbles or in damp peat.
FEEDING Weekly in spring when buds are forming.
PROPAGATION From cuttings of half-ripened wood in summer.
FLOWERING SEASON April–September.

CALADIUM · *Araceae*

Highly decorative foliage plants with large arrow-shaped leaves of white, cream, pink and crimson on long, delicate stems. Height up to 40 cm (16 in). Dry the plant out at the end of the season and start into growth again, one to three tubers to a pot, in spring.

COMPOST Rich, peat-based.
TEMPERATURE Warm: 21–24°C (70–75°F) in spring and summer; overwinter tubers at about 12°C (54°F). When starting plants into growth a temperature of 24–26°C (75–79°F), in a damp situation, is needed, but move to a cooler place when leaves sprout.
LIGHT A shady place, ideally in a plant window or terrarium.
WATER Generously in spring and summer, sparingly from late summer until the leaves shrivel.
HUMIDITY High; place pots in moist peat and spray frequently if not in an enclosed plant window or terrarium.
FEEDING Weekly in the growing season, April–August. A spray-on foliar feed is good.
PROPAGATION From small offsets with young leaves, in March at 18°C (64°F).

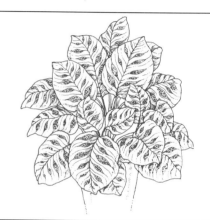

CALATHEA · *Marantaceae*

Variegated foliage plants with some of the most beautiful leaf patterns, up to 60 cm (2 ft) in height. These plants, like caladium, do best in a plant window or terrarium where they can make their own humid micro-climate. *C. lancifolia* or *C. ornata* would be a good choice.

COMPOST Loam-based.
TEMPERATURE Warm; in winter 16–18°C (61–64°F).
LIGHT A shady place, ideally in an enclosed plant window.
WATER Keep moist.
HUMIDITY High; spray frequently and stand pots in moist peat.
FEEDING Fortnightly June–September.
PROPAGATION By division of the roots in early summer.

CAMPANULA ISOPHYLLA · *Campanulaceae*

A trailing plant with pale blue or white flowers, star- or bell-shaped. Height 15 cm (6 in), spread 30–45 cm (12–18 in).

COMPOST Loam-based.
TEMPERATURE Round about 16°C (61°F); 7°C (45°F) in winter.
LIGHT Bright, but not in hot summer sun.
WATER Moderate to generous from April to October, depending on how warm and how dry it is; little in winter.
HUMIDITY Stand on trays of moist pebbles and spray occasionally.
FEEDING Every 2 weeks in the growing season, April–October.
PROPAGATION From 5 cm (2 in) tip cuttings in spring, rooted at 18°C (64°F), three cuttings to a pot.
FLOWERING SEASON July–October.

CAPSICUM · *Solanaceae* · Ornamental Pepper

There are a number of annual peppers and chillies grown for their decorative fruits, as well as the edible varieties. 45 cm (18 in) tall.

COMPOST Loam-based.
TEMPERATURE Any normal room, though it does better if it is on the cool side.
LIGHT Good bright light, but out of direct sun.
WATER Generously, but allow the compost to dry out before watering again.
HUMIDITY Spray from time to time.
FEEDING Every 2 weeks while fruits are forming.
PROPAGATION From seed sown in spring.
FLOWERING SEASON Fruits September–January.

CAREX · *Cyperaceae* · Sedge

Tufts of grass-like leaves growing in fountains, sometimes variegated, 20–30 cm (8–12 in) high.

COMPOST Loam-based.
TEMPERATURE Moderate to cool; 8–16°C (46–61°F) in winter.
LIGHT A good light out of direct sun.
WATER Keep moist, never wet.
HUMIDITY Average; spray occasionally.
FEEDING Fortnightly in the growing season, April–August.
PROPAGATION By division or from seed in spring.

CEPHALOCEREUS · *Cactaceae* · Old Man Cactus

Columnar cacti; *C. senilis* is covered with soft white hairs. Height 8–45 cm (3–18 in).

COMPOST Loam, peat and sharp sand, or special cactus mix.
TEMPERATURE Very warm in summer; ideally not below 15°C (59°F) in winter, though it will survive a lower temperature.
LIGHT Bright and sunny.
WATER Moderate in summer, almost dry in winter.
HUMIDITY None; keep dry.
FEEDING Every 2–3 weeks April–September.
PROPAGATION From offsets or from seed in summer.

CEREUS · *Cactaceae*

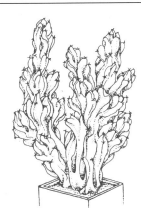

Branching columns, some with a decorative blue, waxy bloom. Height ranges from 5–8 cm (2–3 in) to 50 cm (20 in).

COMPOST Loam, peat and sharp sand, or special cactus mix.
TEMPERATURE Very warm in summer; cool (6°C/43°F) in winter.
LIGHT Bright, sunny, well-ventilated.
WATER Occasionally in summer; keep virtually dry in winter.
HUMIDITY None; spray to remove dust occasionally.
FEEDING Every 2–3 weeks April–September.
PROPAGATION By rooting sections, or from seed, in April.

CEROPEGIA · *Asclepiadaceae*

Succulent plants with very small leaves strung like beads along the fine hanging stems. Good for hanging baskets or on a high shelf. Stems and flowers are purplish, as are the undersides of the leaves.

COMPOST Peat mix, or loam, peat and sharp sand.
TEMPERATURE Very warm in summer, cool in winter.
LIGHT Good and bright, in the sun.
WATER Very little; sparingly in summer, even less in winter.
HUMIDITY None; keep dry.
FEEDING Every 2–3 weeks April–August.
PROPAGATION By division or from stem cuttings in summer (left to dry for a few days before rooting). Tiny tubers develop along the stems, and these can be detached and potted at 18°C (64°F).
FLOWERING SEASON June–August.

CHAMAECEREUS · *Cactaceae* · **Peanut Cactus**

One of the easiest cacti to grow and propagate, growing flat in long sausage shapes, and producing huge red flowers. Only 5 cm (2 in) high, but spreads to 30 cm (1 ft).

COMPOST Loam-based with added grit, or special cactus mix.
TEMPERATURE Very warm in summer, cool in winter, not above 10°C (50°F) if possible.
LIGHT Full sun and plenty of light.
WATER Plenty in summer, very little in winter.
HUMIDITY None; keep dry.
FEEDING Every 2 or 3 weeks April–August.
PROPAGATION Sections will root easily in summer.
FLOWERING SEASON May–August.

CHAMAEDOREA · *Palmaceae* · **Parlour Palm**

One of the easiest as well as one of the most elegant house palms, suitable for most rooms. *C. elegans*, also called *Neanthe elegans* and sometimes sold as *Neanthe bella*, has long fronds of pointed leaves. Height up to 1.2 m (4 ft), usually sold at 30 cm (1 ft).

COMPOST Peat or loam.
TEMPERATURE Normal living room, ideally 14–16°C (57–61°F) in summer; in winter 10–12°C (50–54°F).
LIGHT Good to moderate; out of bright sunlight.
WATER Keep compost always just moist.
HUMIDITY Spray daily if in a warm dry room, otherwise occasionally.
FEEDING Weak fertilizer fortnightly April–August.
PROPAGATION From seed in summer.

CHAMAEROPS HUMILIS · *Palmaceae* · **European Fan Palm**

A palm, hardy in temperate gardens, which is also sold small as a houseplant. Grows to 1 m (3 ft) in a pot.

COMPOST Loam-based.
TEMPERATURE Warm in summer (outside if possible); very cool (4°C/39°F) in winter.
LIGHT Good bright light in an airy situation; out of direct sun.
WATER Generously in summer, very little in winter.
HUMIDITY Average; spray occasionally.
FEEDING Fortnightly in the growing season, April–August.
PROPAGATION From suckers taken from the base of the plant in autumn.

CHLOROPHYTUM COMOSUM · *Liliaceae* · Spider Plant

A well-known and deservedly popular creeping and trailing houseplant with rosettes of pointed leaves, green and white striped in *C. c.* 'Variegatum', and 20–40 cm (8–16 in) long.

COMPOST Either peat or loam.
TEMPERATURE Almost any; winter minimum 7°C (45°F).
LIGHT Bright or fairly bright; also tolerant of fairly dark places.
WATER Generously in summer, less in winter.
HUMIDITY Does best in moist warmth; spray frequently.
FEEDING Every 2 weeks March–September.
PROPAGATION Baby plantlets form at the end of the flowering stem, and these are easily removed and potted. Large clumps can be divided. This is best done in summer.

CHRYSALIDOCARPUS LUTESCENS · *Palmaceae* · Areca or Butterfly Palm

Delicate palms with fronds of long, narrow leaflets. It grows to 6 m (20 ft) and more, but pot plants are usually 1.2–2.5 m (4–8 ft).

COMPOST Loam-based.
TEMPERATURE Very warm all the year round; it really likes a daytime temperature of 24–29°C (75–84°F) and a nighttime temperature of 16°C (61°F), but will survive in a normal room provided it doesn't get too cold.
LIGHT Slightly shaded from the sun.
WATER Generous all the year round.
HUMIDITY High; spray frequently and place pot on damp pebbles or in moist peat.
FEEDING Fortnightly April–August.
PROPAGATION From ripe seeds in spring.

CHRYSANTHEMUM · *Compositae*

Well-known flowering plants, up to 45–60 cm (18–24 in) high but usually about 30 cm (12 in), produced by the growers as all-the-year-round plants and as a result disposable. You can cut the plant down to 5 cm (2 in) in late autumn, but flowering in subsequent years is rarely satisfactory.

COMPOST Keep in the pot it is bought in, usually peat-based.
TEMPERATURE Cool and airy.
LIGHT Bright, but away from direct sun.
WATER Generous.
HUMIDITY Moderate; spray occasionally.
FEEDING Not necessary as plants are disposable.
PROPAGATION Rarely possible, though you can try stem cuttings from young shoots in spring.
FLOWERING SEASON All the year round.

CINERARIA · *Compositae*

Popular flowering plants 35–70 cm (14–28 in) tall with vivid red, pink, purple or white 'daisy' flowers, sold in winter and spring. Like flowering chrysanthemums they are disposable and discarded when flowering is over.

COMPOST As bought. Peat-based if grown from seed.
TEMPERATURE Cool.
LIGHT Away from direct sun; a north window would be suitable.
WATER Keep damp.
HUMIDITY Average; spray occasionally.
FEEDING Not necessary.
PROPAGATION From seed in spring.
FLOWERING SEASON November–April.

CISSUS · *Vitaceae* · Kangaroo Vine

A very easy evergreen climbing plant with toothed leaves. *C. antarctica* is happy in most rooms. Climbing to 2 m (7 ft) or more.

COMPOST Loam-based.
TEMPERATURE Cool; it can survive as low as 5°C (41°F) in winter, and ideally temperature should never be higher than 18°C (64°F).
LIGHT Good, but out of direct sun.
WATER Generously in summer, letting the compost dry out between waterings; keep just moist in winter.
HUMIDITY Not demanding; spray occasionally in dry rooms.
FEEDING Fortnightly March–September.
PROPAGATION From stem cuttings rooted in late spring at 18–21°C (64–70°F), or from leaf cuttings.

CITRUS · *Rutaceae* · Decorative Orange and Lemon Trees

These are usually bought with flowers and fruit; they can be grown from pips but in this case will be unlikely to flower or fruit. The commonest are *C. limon* (lemon) and *C. mitis*, the calamondin orange. They are best bought in late spring. Height 30–90 cm (1–3 ft).

COMPOST Loam-based, well-drained.
TEMPERATURE Normal room; winter minimum 12°C (54°F).
LIGHT Slightly shaded in summer; bright and sunny the rest of the year. Ideally put outside in summer.
WATER Keep moist but never wet in summer; water sparsely in winter.
HUMIDITY Spray frequently in warm conditions, or stand on moist pebbles or in damp peat.
FEEDING Once a month April–September.
PROPAGATION Try sowing seeds in spring or summer.
FLOWERING SEASON May–September.

CLIVIA MINIATA · *Amaryllidaceae* · Kaffir Lily

A long-lived flowering plant with strap-like evergreen leaves and orange flowers in spring. Grows to 45 cm (18 in).

COMPOST Loam-based.
TEMPERATURE Ordinary room temperature; in autumn and early winter cool, 10–15°C (50–59°F).
LIGHT Good, but not in full sun; an east window is ideal.
WATER Keep moist from March to September; give very little in winter.
HUMIDITY Not necessary to spray; keep leaves wiped clean.
FEEDING Once or twice a month March–September.
PROPAGATION From offsets after flowering.
FLOWERING SEASON February–April.

COCOS WEDDELIANA · *Palmaceae* · Dwarf Coconut Palm

A small-scale palm for smaller rooms, with long, delicate, tapering, pinnate leaflets. Up to 1.2 m (4 ft) high. Also known as microcoelum, or *Syagrus weddeliana*.

COMPOST Loam-based, with sharp sand and peat added.
TEMPERATURE Warm in summer; not below 18°C (64°F) in winter.
LIGHT Avoid direct sunlight; any good to average light will do.
WATER Keep moist all the year round, leaving a little water in the saucer at all times.
HUMIDITY Mist-spray occasionally, and stand pot on moist pebbles or in damp peat.
FEEDING Every 2 weeks April–September.
PROPAGATION From seed in spring.

CODIAEUM · *Euphorbiaceae* · Croton

Brightly coloured evergreen plants with leaves marbled, veined or spotted in green, red, white, pink, yellow and brown, growing to 30–90 cm (1–3 ft).

COMPOST Loam-based.
TEMPERATURE Average; 16–18°C (61–64°F) in winter.
LIGHT Good, but out of direct sun.
WATER Keep moist in spring and summer; water very sparingly in autumn and winter.
HUMIDITY Spray occasionally.
FEEDING Fortnightly in the growing season, April–August.
PROPAGATION Not worth attempting.

COELOGYNE · *Orchidaceae*

This evergreen tree orchid from East Asia is one of the easiest to grow in the house. With pairs of strap-like leaves and pendulous flowers, it is best in a hanging basket. It flowers in winter and spring, with white, yellow or pink blooms.

COMPOST Orchid compost or sphagnum moss and osmunda fibre mixture.
TEMPERATURE Cool; in winter 14–15°C (57–59°F).
LIGHT Bright but out of direct sun, e.g. an east-facing window.
WATER Average in summer; the bare minimum in winter.
HUMIDITY Stand pot on moist pebbles or in damp peat, and spray daily May–August.
FEEDING Fortnightly from when buds first appear until they stop appearing.
PROPAGATION By root division in spring.
FLOWERING SEASON December–March.

COFFEA ARABICA · *Rubiaceae* · Arabian Coffee Plant

The small coffee tree or bush grows up to 2 m (7 ft) in a greenhouse but is usually 60–80 cm (24–32 in) as a houseplant. The glossy leaves have wavy edges.

COMPOST Loam-based.
TEMPERATURE Warm; cooler in winter, 15–20°C (59–68°F); soil temperature not below 16°C (61°F).
LIGHT Semi-shade in summer, brighter in winter.
WATER Generous in summer, sparing in winter, but do not let the soil ball dry out.
HUMIDITY Average; spray occasionally.
FEEDING Fortnightly April–August.
PROPAGATION From seed in spring (see p. 43), or from cuttings of side-shoots with a heel in late summer.

COLEUS · *Labiatae* · Flame Nettle

Richly coloured and patterned foliage plants in various combinations of yellow, red, green, and velvet-brown. Usually treated as annuals and discarded. 30–60 cm (1–2 ft). (See also p. 46.)

COMPOST Peat-based.
TEMPERATURE Normal room.
LIGHT Good light is essential for the bright colours. Put on a sunny sill, but shade from the hottest sun. Ideally put outside in summer.
WATER Keep moist.
HUMIDITY Mist-spray daily.
FEEDING Every 2 weeks April–September.
PROPAGATION From cuttings of shoot tips in spring or late summer, or from seed sown from February to April (see p. 43).

CORDYLINE · *Liliaceae* · Cabbage Palm

Shrubs from south-east Asia and Australia; *C. terminalis* has long pointed leaves in a dramatic range of colours, bronzy purple and red. *C. australis* is a tougher plant than most of the others. Grows from 30 cm (1 ft) to 1 m (3 ft) or more. (See also p. 48.)

COMPOST Peat- or loam-based.
TEMPERATURE Minimum 12°C (54°F); 21°C (70°F) is ideal throughout the year.
LIGHT Bright, but shaded from the hottest sun in summer.
WATER Freely in spring and summer, keeping the compost always moist; water only when the soil is dry in autumn and winter.
HUMIDITY Give a fine mist-spray daily, or stand pots on trays of moist pebbles or in damp peat.
FEEDING Every 2 weeks April–August.
PROPAGATION From suckers in spring, or from seeds sown at 18–21°C (64–70°F).

CRASSULA · *Crassulaceae* · Jade Tree

A large family of leaf succulents, all worth having. *C. arborescens* is like a plump miniature tree with jade-like shiny leaves. *C. argentea* is a very similar plant, also known as the jade tree. 15 cm–1 m (6 in–3 ft).

COMPOST Loam-based with added coarse sand or grit.
TEMPERATURE As hot as possible from spring to autumn; from October to March not above 10°C (50°F), and will survive 4°C (39°F).
LIGHT Bright and sunny.
WATER Water moderately from April to September, then gradually less till you are giving hardly any in winter.
HUMIDITY Not necessary as they like being dry.
FEEDING Every 2–3 weeks April–September.
PROPAGATION By rooting leaves or small shoots in spring or summer, after letting them dry or 'callus' for a few days.

CRYPTANTHUS · *Bromeliaceae* · Earth Stars

Small, flat bromeliads like tabby starfish, excellent in flat dish arrangements. Up to 30 cm (1 ft) across.

COMPOST Peat-based.
TEMPERATURE Not below 16°C (61°F) if possible.
LIGHT Bright, but out of direct sun.
WATER Keep moist at all times, but never wet.
HUMIDITY High; mist-spray frequently, and stand pot on moist pebbles or in damp peat. Excellent in bottle gardens or terrariums.
FEEDING Once a month April–September.
PROPAGATION From offsets taken in spring and summer and rooted at 21°C (70°F).

CYCLAMEN · *Primulaceae*

Popular winter-flowering plants with flower colours ranging from pure white to deep crimson, and beautiful silver markings on the leaves; they are sometimes discarded when flowering is over, but can be rested for the summer in a cool place, inside or out, and started into growth again in August. 15–30 cm (6–12 in) high. (See also p. 94.)

COMPOST Peat or loam.
TEMPERATURE Cool; 10–16°C (50–61°F) is ideal.
LIGHT The best possible in winter, but out of full sun.
WATER Water when compost has almost dried out, either from below, putting lukewarm water in the saucer and pouring it away in 20 minutes, or from above, avoiding the corm and foliage. When growing plants may need watering twice a day, but stop watering gradually as leaves yellow. Keep quite dry when resting.
HUMIDITY Moderate; pots can stand in bowls of moist pebbles.
FEEDING Weekly while budding and flowering.
PROPAGATION Not possible in the house.
FLOWERING SEASON November–March.

CYPERUS · *Cyperaceae* · Umbrella Plant

C. alternifolius has tall stems up to 80 cm (32 in) topped by radiating leaves like the spokes of an umbrella. A highly decorative marsh plant.

COMPOST Peat- or loam-based.
TEMPERATURE Normal room; in winter above 10°C (50°F). Very tolerant.
LIGHT Good, in or out of sun.
WATER Soaked throughout the year; in fact the pot can stand in a bowl of water kept topped up.
HUMIDITY Spray daily in spring and summer.
FEEDING Once a fortnight April–September.
PROPAGATION Divide roots in spring, or put the flowering tips of the rosettes head down in water and roots will form.

CYRTOMIUM FALCATUM · *Polypodiaceae* · Holly Fern

Handsome ferns from India, easy in the house, growing up to 60 cm (2 ft). *C.f.* 'Rochfordianum' is the holly fern, rarely growing above 30 cm (1 ft).

COMPOST Peat-based.
TEMPERATURE It prefers cool conditions, but stands normal room temperatures.
LIGHT Ideally bright and sunny, but will tolerate shade.
WATER Keep moist throughout the year.
HUMIDITY Average to low; not fussy.
FEEDING Every 2 weeks April–August.
PROPAGATION Divide large plants in spring.

DAVALLIA · *Davalliaceae*

Ferns with finely dissected fronds reaching 30–45 cm (12–18 in). *D. bullata* (syn. *D. mariesii*) is the squirrel's foot fern.

COMPOST Peat-based.
TEMPERATURE Warm in summer, 14°C (57°F) in winter.
LIGHT Shade.
WATER Generous in summer, sparing in winter.
HUMIDITY Average to high, according to temperature; spray frequently and place pots on damp pebbles or gravel or in moist peat.
FEEDING Once a month April–September.
PROPAGATION By division, or from cuttings of the rhizomes in early spring.

DIEFFENBACHIA · *Araceae* · Dumb Cane

A very easy and adaptable houseplant with large, imposing marbled leaves. Leaves and stems contain a poison. Grows to 1 m (3 ft) or more. (See also p. 69.)

COMPOST Any, peat- or loam-based, with added sand for drainage.
TEMPERATURE Ordinary living room; in winter not below 15–16°C (59–61°F).
LIGHT Slightly shaded in summer; brighter in autumn and winter.
WATER Keep evenly moist throughout the year.
HUMIDITY High; mist-spray daily, and stand on tray of moist pebbles or in damp peat.
FEEDING Once every 2 weeks April–August.
PROPAGATION Growing tips can be rooted in a propagator at 18–21°C (64–70°F) in gritty compost.

DIZYGOTHECA · *Araliaceae* · Finger Aralia or False Aralia

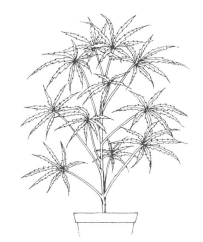

One of the most elegant of plants, with thin leaves with saw edges, maturing from coppery green to purple to near black. Grows up to 1.2 m (4 ft) high.

COMPOST Peat- or loam-based.
TEMPERATURE 18°C (64°F) all the time would be ideal; not below 12–16°C (54–61°F) in winter.
LIGHT As good a light as possible in winter; away from direct sun in summer.
WATER Keep just moist from April to August; in winter water only when the compost feels dry, but be careful not to let root ball dry out.
HUMIDITY Plenty; mist-spray daily, and if possible put the pot on moist pebbles or in a larger container packed around with damp peat or moss.
FEEDING Young plants that are potted on every year will not need feeding; mature plants should be fed every 2 weeks from March or April to August.
PROPAGATION Not easy.

DRACAENA · *Liliaceae*

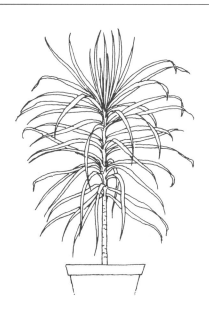

Several of these splendid palm-like plants are sold as houseplants, *D. fragrans* with fine curving leaves, *D. deremensis* with a rosette of sword-shaped leaves striped green and silver, and, perhaps the best of all and certainly one of the easiest of all plants, *D. marginata*. Height up to 1–2 m (3–7 ft). *D. sanderiana* is smaller – about 45 cm (18 in) high – and does well in an enclosed plant case. (See also p. 48.)

COMPOST Peat- or loam-based.
TEMPERATURE Ordinary living room; winter night temperature not below 10–12°C (50–54°F).
LIGHT Good – as much as possible in winter, but out of the sun in summer – but very tolerant.
WATER Keep moist from spring to autumn; in winter only water when the compost is dry.
HUMIDITY Mist-spray daily in summer or if in a dry atmosphere.
FEEDING Every 2 weeks April–August.
PROPAGATION From tip cuttings rooted at 21°C (70°F) in spring; stems of old plants cut into (8 cm) 3 in sections will also root.

Drejerella see **Beloperone.**

ECHEVERIA · *Crassulaceae*

A group of succulent plants from South and Central America, forming rosettes of various types, with grey-green leaves, often with a white waxy sheen. Some are borne 45 cm (18 in) high on stems, but most grow almost on the ground. Red, orange or white flowers on long stems appear in summer.

COMPOST Free-draining, loam-based, with grit or sand added.
TEMPERATURE Very warm from spring to autumn; October to March not above 10°C (50°F).
LIGHT Plenty; in full sun in summer.
WATER Plenty in the growing period; keep barely moist in winter.
HUMIDITY None; likes being dry.
FEEDING Every 2–3 weeks April–August.
PROPAGATION From young offset rosettes, leaf cuttings or seed, in spring and summer.
FLOWERING SEASON June–August.

ECHINOCACTUS · *Cactaceae*

Spherical or cylindrical cacti divided by spiny ribs, some reaching 15 cm (6 in) in diameter.

COMPOST Two parts loam to one part sharp sand, or cactus mix.
TEMPERATURE Very warm in summer, not below 10°C (50°F) in winter.
LIGHT Good bright light, shaded from direct sunlight in spring.
WATER Keep moist in summer, virtually dry in winter.
HUMIDITY None; spray occasionally to remove dust.
FEEDING Every 2–3 weeks April–August.
PROPAGATION From seed in spring.

ECHINOCEREUS · *Cactaceae*

Low-growing columnar branched cacti, producing large pink or purple flowers in June and July. Height 5–10 cm (2–4 in).

COMPOST Loam and sharp sand, or cactus mix.
TEMPERATURE Very warm in summer, cool in winter.
LIGHT Bright and sunny, with plenty of air.
WATER Keep moist in summer, virtually dry in winter.
HUMIDITY None; spray occasionally to remove dust.
FEEDING Every 2–3 weeks April–August.
PROPAGATION From stem cuttings in spring or summer, or seed sown in early spring at 21°C (70°F).
FLOWERING SEASON June and July.

ECHINOPSIS · *Cactaceae* · Sea Urchin Cactus

Small globular cacti producing beautiful flowers of scarlet, yellow, pink or white. Usually 10–15 cm (4–6 in), but can reach 30 cm (1 ft).

COMPOST A rich humusy mixture plus some sharp sand, or cactus mix.
TEMPERATURE Very warm in summer, cool in winter.
LIGHT Bright and sunny.
WATER Quite generous in summer; keep dryish in winter.
HUMIDITY None; keep dry, but spray occasionally to remove dust.
FEEDING Every 2–3 weeks April–August.
PROPAGATION From offsets (baby cacti), or from seed, in spring or summer.
FLOWERING SEASON June–August.

EUONYMUS JAPONICUS · *Celastraceae*

A very neat pot plant with glossy, laurel-like leaves, sometimes variegated. 30–90 cm (1–3 ft) is the usual height, though it could ultimately reach 2 m (6–7 ft). Plants should be cut back well in spring.

COMPOST Loam-based.
TEMPERATURE Cool; in winter 4–6°C (39–43°F), outside if possible in summer.
LIGHT A good light, and a well ventilated position, not close to other plants.
WATER Generously in summer, sparingly in winter.
HUMIDITY Average; spray occasionally, and wash leaves to remove dust.
FEEDING Fortnightly April–August.
PROPAGATION From shoot tips in spring.

EUPHORBIA · *Euphorbiaceae* · Poinsettia, Crown of Thorns, and others

The euphorbias include several well-known – and very different – houseplants. Undoubtedly the best-known is *E. pulcherrima*, or poinsettia, with its bright red decorative bracts. Usually regarded as disposable, as it is not that easy to bring through the year to 'flower' again. Up to 1 m (3 ft) tall.

   E. milii is another very decorative shrub, spiny, with small green leaves and brilliant red bracts; it is known as the crown of thorns and can flower throughout the year. Grows to 1 m (3 ft). (See also p. 64.)

   Many of the euphorbias are succulents, most of these containing a milky white juice which can irritate the skin. *E. pseudocactus* looks like a jointed cactus (15–30 cm/6–12 in high). *E. caput-medusae* has snake-like branches growing from a short stem (15 cm/6 in). *E. obesa* is spherical (5–10 cm/2–4 in).

E. pulcherrima

COMPOST Peat-based; but for plants treated as temporary houseplants, whatever compost they are bought in.
TEMPERATURE 12–18°C (54–64°F) is ideal, but they will be alright in any normal room.
LIGHT Bright and sunny in winter, but shade from summer sun.
WATER Keep always moist.
HUMIDITY Not important.
FEEDING Not necessary for temporary houseplants. Feed rooted cuttings every week for 6 months, starting when shoots first appear.
PROPAGATION From 8 cm (3 in) tip cuttings in summer rooted at 18°C (64°F).
FLOWERING SEASON October–March.

E. milii

COMPOST Free-draining, loam-based, with grit or sand added.
TEMPERATURE From spring to autumn full sun and heat, October–March not above 10°C (50°F).
LIGHT Bright and sunny.
WATER Moderately in summer, just enough to keep root ball from drying out in winter.
HUMIDITY None; keep dry.
FEEDING Fortnightly April–August.
PROPAGATION Stem cuttings root easily.
FLOWERING SEASON All the year round.

Succulent species

CARE As for Echinopsis.

EXACUM AFFINE · *Gentianaceae* · Persian Violet

A small bushy annual, available in summer, and discarded when flowering finishes. About 15 cm (6 in) high. The flowers are purple-blue with yellow centres and sweetly scented.

COMPOST Peat- or loam-based.
TEMPERATURE Moderate to cool.
LIGHT Good, but out of direct sun.
WATER Keep moist.
HUMIDITY Average; spray occasionally.
FEEDING Fortnightly.
PROPAGATION From seed sown in spring at 20–24°C (68–75°F).
FLOWERING SEASON June–October.

X FATSHEDERA · *Araliaceae* · Ivy Tree

A very popular houseplant, a cross between *Fatsia japonica* and *Hedera helix* (ivy). It is a climbing plant, but needs support; it has star-shaped leaves. Reaches 1–2 m (3–7 ft).

COMPOST Loam-based.
TEMPERATURE Must be cool in winter; a hall or porch is ideal.
LIGHT Light shade; also does well in a low light.
WATER Plenty from March to September; in winter only when the compost feels dry.
HUMIDITY Spray frequently, and keep leaves wiped clean.
FEEDING Every 2 weeks April–August.
PROPAGATION From 10–13 cm (4–5 in) stem cuttings, rooted at 18°C (64°F) in a propagator.

FATSIA JAPONICA · *Araliaceae*

A very easy houseplant with glossy green palmate leaves; hardy outside in summer. Height 1 m (3 ft).

COMPOST Loam-based.
TEMPERATURE Will tolerate almost any, but prefers to be cool.
LIGHT Tolerates low light, but likes good light, though not direct sun.
WATER Keep always moist in summer; allow to dry out between waterings in winter.
HUMIDITY Not necessary; spray occasionally to keep leaves clean.
FEEDING Every 2 weeks April–August.
PROPAGATION From seed sown in spring at 18–24°C (64–75°F) (see p. 43).

FEROCACTUS · *Cactaceae*

Spherical and cylindrical cacti, usually with long, decorative spines and orange or yellow flowers. Height 15–30 cm (6–12 in).

COMPOST Loam, peat and sharp sand or special cactus mix.
TEMPERATURE Very warm in summer; cool (8–10°C/46–50°F) in winter.
LIGHT As well lit as possible, in the sun. Put outside in summer if you can.
WATER Average in summer; keep dry in winter.
HUMIDITY None.
FEEDING Every 2–3 weeks April–August.
PROPAGATION From seed in spring.
FLOWERING SEASON July and August.

FICUS · *Moraceae* · Rubber Plant, Weeping Fig, and others

F. elastica, the rubber plant, has always been an extremely popular houseplant; it can reach as much as 3 m (10 ft). *F. benjamina*, known as the weeping fig, a graceful tree with delicate, pointed leaves and arching branches, is another of the most popular species. Height up to 2 m (7 ft).

COMPOST Peat- or loam-based.
TEMPERATURE Normal room temperatures. For *F. elastica* a minimum winter temperature of 16°C (61°F) is ideal, but it will tolerate 12°C (54°F); *F. benjamina* also needs a minimum of 12°C (54°F).
LIGHT Moderate; out of direct sun.
WATER Keep moist from spring to autumn; let soil dry out between waterings in winter.
HUMIDITY Keep warm and moist; mist-spray frequently, and stand on moist pebbles or in damp peat if the room is warm.
FEEDING Feed every 2 weeks April–August.
PROPAGATION *F. elastica* from leaf cuttings and air layering; *F. benjamina* from air layering. This can be done at any time of year given a temperature of 18°C (64°F).

FITTONIA · *Acanthaceae*

A low-growing foliage plant with decorative veining patterns – green, pink, purple, or silver. Ideal for bottle gardens and terrariums. Grows to 20 cm (8 in).

COMPOST Peat- or loam-based.
TEMPERATURE Warm to normal; in winter not below 12°C (54°F).
LIGHT Keep out of direct sunlight. Light shade might be ideal in summer, with slightly more light in winter.
WATER Keep moist but not waterlogged in summer; water more sparingly in winter.
HUMIDITY High; spray daily. Put in another pot, filled with peat, or grow in a terrarium.
FEEDING Every 2 weeks from March to August unless in a closed case.
PROPAGATION From tip cuttings in spring or summer rooted at 21°C (70°F), or by division of the roots in summer.

FUCHSIA · *Oenotheraceae*

Flowering shrubs from Central and South America popular as flowering houseplants both for window boxes and hanging baskets and for pots in the house. Height 60–90 cm (2–3 ft).

COMPOST Loam-based.
TEMPERATURE Warm in summer, 10–12°C (50–54°F) in winter.
LIGHT Semi-shade in a well-ventilated place.
WATER Keep moist in spring and summer; water very sparingly in winter.
HUMIDITY Spray frequently in summer, and stand in damp peat or on moist pebbles.
FEEDING Fortnightly during the growing season – April till the end of the summer.
PROPAGATION From stem cuttings in spring or late summer.
FLOWERING SEASON May–September.

GASTERIA · *Liliaceae*

A large genus of succulents with thick, fleshy leaves patterned with white growing in a fan or rosette, and red flowers in spring or summer. 8–30 cm (3–12 in) high.

COMPOST Loam-based with sand added.
TEMPERATURE Very warm in summer, cool in winter.
LIGHT Full sun and bright light.
WATER Plenty of water in summer, little in winter.
HUMIDITY None.
FEEDING Every 2–3 weeks April–August.
PROPAGATION From offsets, which are freely produced, in spring or summer.
FLOWERING SEASON May–July.
NOTE Haworthia is a very similar plant, to be cared for in exactly the same way.

Geranium see **Pelargonium.**

Gloxinia see **Sinningia.**

GREVILLEA ROBUSTA · *Proteaceae* · Silky Oak

An evergreen shrub with feathery foliage growing 1–2 m (3–7 ft) as a pot plant.

COMPOST Loam- or peat-based.
TEMPERATURE Cool; 6–10°C (43–50°F) in winter, outside in summer if possible.
LIGHT Semi-shade in summer, sunny in winter.
WATER Moderate all the year round.
HUMIDITY Spray occasionally.
FEEDING Every 2–3 weeks April–August.
PROPAGATION From seed in spring at 18–24°C (64–75°F) (see p. 43).

GYNURA · *Compositae* · Velvet Plant

One of the best purple-red plants, growing to 1 m (3 ft). The leaves are covered in soft hairs, which gives them a velvety sheen. Pinch out the young flowering stems to make the plant bushy.

COMPOST Loam-based.
TEMPERATURE Warm throughout the year; not below 10°C (50°F) in winter.
LIGHT Sunny and bright in winter, but out of the hottest sun in summer.
WATER Generously in summer, sparingly in winter.
HUMIDITY Spray occasionally, but not when plant is in full sun.
FEEDING Fortnightly April–August.
PROPAGATION From 8 cm (3 in) tip cuttings in April, rooted in water or compost at 18°C (64°F).

HEDERA HELIX · *Araliaceae* · Ivy

Hardy evergreen plants, climbing or trailing, with pretty three- or five-lobed leaves, sometimes marked in yellow, cream or light green. They make easy houseplants for cool places. Will grow to 2–4 m (7–12 ft).

COMPOST Peat- or loam-based.
TEMPERATURE 18°C (64°F) is ideal in summer; cool in winter.
LIGHT A good light out of direct sun, or half-shady position.
WATER Keep just moist in spring and summer; water more sparingly in winter.
HUMIDITY Spray frequently and give plenty of fresh air.
FEEDING Fortnightly April–August.
PROPAGATION 8 cm (3 in) tip cuttings root easily in gritty soil or water at any time.

HELXINE · _Urticaceae_ · Mind Your Own Business

A creeping plant for greenhouse ground cover or for hanging pots.

COMPOST Loam-based.
TEMPERATURE Moderate in summer, cool in winter.
LIGHT Good light, out of direct sun.
WATER Generous in summer, sparing in winter.
HUMIDITY Average; spray occasionally.
FEEDING Fortnightly April–August.
PROPAGATION Stem cuttings root easily in early summer.

HEPTAPLEURUM · _Araliaceae_ · Umbrella Tree

Close relatives of schefflera (heptapleurum is a subgenus of schefflera), and often sold as schefflera, these are quick-growing and imposing houseplants, with long-stemmed palmate leaves. They can reach small tree proportions (30 cm–2 m/1–7 ft).

COMPOST Loam-based.
TEMPERATURE Around 18°C (64°F); not below 10°C (50°F) in winter.
LIGHT A good light, but shade from hottest sun in summer; an east or west window is ideal.
WATER Very thirsty in summer; let the soil almost dry out between waterings in winter.
HUMIDITY Spray frequently.
FEEDING Every 2 weeks April–September.
PROPAGATION From seed sown in spring at 21°C (70°F); stem cuttings also root easily in water.

HIBISCUS · _Malvaceae_ · Chinese Rose

A member of the mallow family growing up to 1 m (3 ft), with dramatic trumpet-shaped flowers with protruding stamens, in orange, pink and crimson; these last only a day but are constantly replaced during the flowering period by fresh buds. It can be pruned after its winter rest.

COMPOST Loam-based.
TEMPERATURE Warm in summer, moderate in winter (12–15°C/54–59°F).
LIGHT A good light, but out of direct sun.
WATER Generously in summer, twice a day if necessary; less in autumn and winter.
HUMIDITY Spray occasionally in summer.
FEEDING Every 2 weeks April–September.
PROPAGATION From tip cuttings in early summer rooted at 24–26°C (75–79°F).
FLOWERING SEASON July–October.

HIPPEASTRUM · _Amaryllidaceae_ · Amaryllis

Bulbs of this beautiful flowering plant can be kept for many years; they can be put in compost as early as November, although they bloom naturally in spring or early summer and are usually started into growth in January, February or March. Stems reach 45–60 cm (18–24 in). (See also p. 11.)

COMPOST Any good compost will do.
TEMPERATURE 16–21°C (61–70°F) when starting bulbs into growth, 10–12°C (50–54°F) when resting.
LIGHT The brightest possible; a sunny sill is ideal.
WATER Keep moist until September or October when the foliage begins to die down.
HUMIDITY Spray occasionally.
FEEDING Every 2 weeks after flowering until September or October.
PROPAGATION Sometimes bulbils appear on the parent plant, and these can be potted on singly.
FLOWERING SEASON February–May.

HOWEA · *Palmaceae*

The archetypal palm; the easiest and one of the most graceful for the house. 30 cm–1.5 m (1–5 ft). Also known as the kentia palm.

COMPOST Loam-based.
TEMPERATURE Normal room, up to 23°C (74°F); can survive 12°C (54°F) in winter, but ideally not below 14–16°C (57–61°F).
LIGHT A good bright light out of direct sun, or semi-shade.
WATER Keep moist all the year round; water more freely in summer.
HUMIDITY Spray leaves daily.
FEEDING Every 2 weeks April–August.
PROPAGATION From seed in early spring in a propagator at 26°C (79°F).

HOYA · *Asclepiadaceae*

Evergreen climbers from the Far East with star-shaped waxy white flowers and fleshy leaves. Of the two species grown in the home, *H. carnosa* is the larger; trained up canes or round wires, it will climb to a metre or so. *H. bella* is smaller, about 23 cm (9 in) high and spreading, and best as a hanging plant. Both these are best in a conservatory but can be kept happy in rooms.

COMPOST Loam- or peat-based.
TEMPERATURE Warm in summer, 10–12°C (50–54°F) in winter.
LIGHT A good light without direct sun.
WATER Moderately in summer, sparingly in winter.
HUMIDITY High; spray frequently in summer, and in winter if the room is warm, and stand pots on damp pebbles or in moist peat.
FEEDING Monthly March–September.
PROPAGATION From stem cuttings rooted in heat in summer.
FLOWERING SEASON May–September.

HYDRANGEA · *Hydrangeaceae*

Popular plants for pots and tubs outside which can also be grown successfully in the house. Bought in flower in the spring they will reach 1 m (3 ft) in a pot. When young the plants should be potted on every spring. The familiar flower clusters are white, pink or blue.

COMPOST Loam-based and lime-free.
TEMPERATURE Cool; in winter 4–8°C (39–46°F).
LIGHT Slightly shaded from the sun.
WATER Generously, twice a day if necessary, with softened or rain water.
HUMIDITY Spray occasionally.
FEEDING Fortnightly March–September.
PROPAGATION Cuttings of young shoots can be rooted under glass in summer.
FLOWERING SEASON May–August.

HYPOESTES · *Acanthaceae*

H. sanguinolenta is a low-growing shrub, with pink-flecked leaves and insignificant lilac flowers; height up to 30 cm (1 ft). *H. aristata* is larger, a bushy plant growing to 30–60 cm (1–2 ft) with pale green leaves.

COMPOST Loam-based,
TEMPERATURE Warm all the year round; 18–20°C (64–68°F) is ideal, but it will do in a normal room. A plant window or terrarium is best.
LIGHT Out of direct sun.
WATER Generously in summer, less in winter. Use soft water.
HUMIDITY High, especially in summer; spray daily and stand on moist pebbles or in damp peat if not in a plant window or terrarium.
FEEDING Fortnightly April–September.
PROPAGATION From seed in spring.

IMPATIENS · *Balsaminaceae* · Busy Lizzie, Balsam

Some of the most popular flowering pot plants, with succulent stems and pink, red, white or striped flowers and green or bronzy leaves. 30 cm (1 ft).

COMPOST Peat or loam.
TEMPERATURE Minimum of 12°C (54°F); it will be happy at 16°C (61°F).
LIGHT A bright and sunny position is ideal, but semi-shade will do.
WATER Generously in spring and summer; keep just moist in winter.
HUMIDITY In warm weather, or if room is warm, stand pots on trays of moist pebbles or in damp peat. Avoid spraying as this can rot the leaves and mark the flowers.
FEEDING Fortnightly May–September.
PROPAGATION Stem or tip cuttings root easily in water or compost at any time, or seed can be sown in spring at 21°C (70°F). Keep seedlings in a bright light.
FLOWERING SEASON All the year round.

IRESINE · *Amaranthaceae*

Brilliant reddish purple-leaved shrubs; *I. herbstii* has dark purple leaves with crimson veins and undersides. 30 cm (1 ft) tall. (See also p. 46.)

COMPOST Loam-based.
TEMPERATURE Warm.
LIGHT A good light is needed to maintain leaf colour and to enable you to see the colour; a sunny sill is ideal.
WATER Generously in summer, less in winter.
HUMIDITY High; stand the pot in moist peat and spray regularly or grow in a terrarium.
FEEDING Fortnightly March–September.
PROPAGATION From stem cuttings in spring and summer.

JASMINUM · *Oleaceae* · Jasmine

Flowering shrubs from China, with small dark green leaves and fragrant star-shaped flowers, white tinged with pink in *J. polyanthum*. Although best in a cool conservatory, they can be grown in a room trained round wires or up trellis. Can grow up to 2 m (6–7 ft) in a year, so keep well pruned. In winter plants must be put in a very cool place.

COMPOST Loam-based.
TEMPERATURE Warm in summer, cool in winter.
LIGHT A good light without direct sun.
WATER Copiously in summer; very little in winter.
HUMIDITY Spray occasionally.
FEEDING Fortnightly August–December.
PROPAGATION From stem cuttings in spring or autumn.
FLOWERING SEASON December–April.

KALANCHOE · *Crassulaceae*

K. blossfeldiana is a popular houseplant, succulent, with long-lasting red, orange or yellow flowers. 30 cm (1 ft) tall.

COMPOST Loam-based, with sharp sand added.
TEMPERATURE Very warm in summer, cool in winter.
LIGHT Bright, but shaded from the hottest summer sun.
WATER Moderately in spring and summer; keep almost dry in winter.
HUMIDITY Keep dry.
FEEDING Every 2–3 weeks April–August.
PROPAGATION From offsets in spring or summer.
FLOWERING SEASON December–May.

LILIUM · *Liliaceae* · Lily

It is not easy to grow lilies in the house but it is worth trying as they make dramatic plants; give them large pots and plenty of space. L.'Enchantment' has orange flowers borne on 60–90 cm (2–3 ft) stems, and specially treated bulbs can be bought to flower in February and March. 'Harmony' has spotted orange flowers in spring, and 'Prosperity' pale yellow flowers also in spring. Untreated bulbs which flower in summer, the more usual lily time, are *L. auratum*, 1.2 m (4 ft) tall with sweet-smelling white trumpet flowers spotted with gold, and *L. regale*, 1 m (3 ft) tall, also with white flowers spotted with gold, purple on the reverse. See p. 25 for planting instructions and more varieties.

COMPOST Loam-based, John Innes No. 1 or 2, with some peat added.
TEMPERATURE Not above 10°C (50°F) immediately after planting; 18–21°C (64–70°F) when buds start to form. Specially prepared bulbs to plant in spring need 20°C (68°F).
LIGHT Bright, but not in direct sun.
WATER Keep moist.
HUMIDITY Low.
FEEDING Every 2 weeks when flower buds show.
PROPAGATION Not possible in the home.
FLOWERING SEASON June–August, except for specially treated bulbs which will flower as early as February.

MAMMILLARIA · *Cactaceae*

The largest and perhaps the most popular genus of cacti; globular, fast-growing but small, and easy to bring into flower. The flowers are white, yellow, mauve or crimson. Height 4–10 cm (1½–4 in).

COMPOST Loam-based, with grit added.
TEMPERATURE Very warm in summer, cool in winter.
LIGHT Bright and sunny.
WATER Moderately in summer, hardly at all in winter.
HUMIDITY None; keep dry.
FEEDING Every 2–3 weeks April–August.
PROPAGATION Separate offsets and pot separately, or sow seed in spring.
FLOWERING SEASON July and August.

MARANTA · *Marantaceae* · Prayer Plant

Among the most beautifully marked leaves of all houseplants. Some have red or white veins, and some have regular brown patches on either side of the central vein. Not easy in normal rooms; a plant window or terrarium is best. Up to 30 cm (1 ft).

COMPOST Loam-based.
TEMPERATURE Daytime 22°C (72°F) in summer, 18–20°C (64–68°F) in winter; at night 16–18°C (61–64°F) in summer, 16°C (61°F) in winter.
LIGHT Good, but out of direct sun.
WATER Generously in summer, less in autumn and winter.
HUMIDITY High; spray frequently and stand pots on moist pebbles or in damp peat if not in a plant window or terrarium.
FEEDING Fortnightly April–September.
PROPAGATION By division when repotting in spring.

Microcoelum see **Cocos weddeliana.**

MILTONIA · *Orchidaceae* · Pansy Orchid

Epiphytic orchids with flat pansy-shaped flowers on arching stems, some flowering in summer, some in autumn. The flowers are yellow, white, pink, red, and purple with exotic markings. Height up to 30 cm (1 ft).

COMPOST Special orchid mix.
TEMPERATURE Cool; 12°C (54°F) in winter, 18°C (64°F) in summer.
LIGHT Slightly away from a window in summer, brighter in winter, but never in direct sun.
WATER In spring and summer generously, sparingly in the resting season.
HUMIDITY High; stand pots in damp peat or on moist pebbles and spray daily in the growing season.
FEEDING Fortnightly in the growing season, April–July, with special orchid food, or as indicated on the label.
PROPAGATION Not possible at home.
FLOWERING SEASON June–October, mostly in the autumn.

MONSTERA DELICIOSA · *Araceae* · Swiss Cheese Plant

Some of the best-known indoor plants, from Mexico. It is known as the Swiss cheese plant because of the holes that develop in the leaves as they mature. Usually grows to 1.8–2.4 m (6–8 ft) high, but can reach as much as 3 m (10 ft). Will in any case need some support. (See also p. 69.)

COMPOST Peat or loam, with added grit or perlite for drainage.
TEMPERATURE Normal room or higher; not lower than 10°C (50°F) in winter.
LIGHT Quite happy in a shady position; keep always out of direct sun.
WATER Freely in spring and summer; keep barely moist in winter.
HUMIDITY High; spray daily with tepid water, and stand on moist pebbles or in damp peat.
FEEDING Every 2 weeks April–August.
PROPAGATION From tip cuttings at 24°C (75°F), or from seed in spring or early summer (see p. 43).

MUSA · *Musaceae* · Banana Palm

Palm-like trees with enormous leaves. Will grow upwards of 1.5 m (5 ft) in 3 years.

COMPOST Peat-based.
TEMPERATURE Warm to average all the year round.
LIGHT Good, but out of direct sun.
WATER Generous in summer, less in winter.
HUMIDITY Spray daily in warm conditions, and stand on moist pebbles or in damp peat.
FEEDING Fortnightly April–August.
PROPAGATION From seed in March or April (see p. 43); grows up to 1 m (3 ft) in the first 6–12 months.

MYRTUS · *Myrtaceae* · Myrtle

An evergreen, scented-leaved hardy shrub. It has masses of tiny cream flowers with prominent stamens in summer. Height 30–60 cm (1–2 ft).

COMPOST Peat-based.
TEMPERATURE Warm in summer, outside if possible; cool (4–6°C/39–43°F) in winter.
LIGHT A good bright light in or out of direct sun, and plenty of fresh air.
WATER Moderate; keep moist with soft (rain) water.
HUMIDITY Moderate; spray occasionally.
FEEDING Fortnightly April–September.
PROPAGATION From stem cuttings in spring and autumn.
FLOWERING SEASON June–August.

NEOREGELIA · *Bromeliaceae*

Rosettes of strap-like leathery leaves, up to 40 cm (16 in) long, some striped, edged or tipped with red, some red in the centre. The central leaves turn red before flowering, and sometimes the whole plant becomes suffused with red.

COMPOST Peat-based, or coarse peat and leaf mould.
TEMPERATURE Normal room; in winter a minimum of around 16°C (61°F).
LIGHT The brightest possible, but out of direct sun.
WATER Keep moist; water less from October to March – just enough to prevent it from drying out. Keep water in the central cup during the growing period; tip it out and replace occasionally.
HUMIDITY Mist-spray daily.
FEEDING Once a month April–September.
PROPAGATION From offshoots in spring rooted at 21°C (70°F) in a propagator.
FLOWERING SEASON Can produce a flower spike at any time of year, and dies after flowering.

NEPHROLEPIS · *Oleandraceae* · **Ladder or Sword Fern**

These ferns have elegant and decorative fronds; they are ideal for hanging baskets or for trailing from pillars or shelves. *N. exaltata* has dark green fronds which reach a length of 1 m (3 ft).

COMPOST Peat or loam.
TEMPERATURE Coolish normal room; not below 10°C (50°F) in winter.
LIGHT Good and bright, but out of direct sun.
WATER Keep moist in growing season; water more sparingly in winter.
HUMIDITY High; mist-spraying daily is essential.
FEEDING Every 2 weeks from April to September.
PROPAGATION By division of the roots in spring or summer. Tips of runners also root easily in moist compost.

NOTOCACTUS · *Cactaceae*

Globular and cylindrical cacti with fine long radiating spines on their ribs and red or yellow flowers. The globular cacti are up to 15 cm (6 in) high, but *N. leninghausii* can reach 1 m (3 ft), and 10 cm (4 in) in diameter.

COMPOST A mixture of loam, peat and sharp sand, or special cactus mix.
TEMPERATURE Very warm in summer, cool in winter (10°C/50°F).
LIGHT Bright and sunny, but it seems to like a little shade in spring; put outdoors in summer if possible.
WATER Keep moist in summer, almost dry in winter.
HUMIDITY Spray on hot days in summer.
FEEDING Every 2–3 weeks April–August.
PROPAGATION From seed in spring.
FLOWERING SEASON July and August.

OPUNTIA · *Cactaceae* · **Prickly Pear**

The famous 'bunny's ears' cactus, with yellow glochids (barbed bristles). They very rarely flower. Up to 30 cm (1 ft) tall.

COMPOST Loam-based with added grit.
TEMPERATURE Very warm in summer, cool in winter.
LIGHT Bright and sunny all the year round.
WATER Moderately in summer, very little in winter.
HUMIDITY None; keep dry.
FEEDING Every 2–3 weeks April–September.
PROPAGATION Sections root easily after a drying off period.

PACHYPHYTUM · *Crassulaceae* · Moon Plant

Succulents related to echeveria, with fleshy leaves, often silver-grey-green with a bloom. Usually up to 30 cm (1 ft) tall. *P. oviferum* sometimes produces red flowers in June.

CARE As for **Echeveria**.

PELARGONIUM · *Geraniaceae* · Geranium, Regal Pelargonium

There is sometimes confusion here as the common geranium (so called because the true geranium is really a hardy perennial) is *P. zonale* or zonal, which has dark 'zone' markings on its leaves, and flowers in white and every shade of red and pink. Then there are the regal pelargoniums, hybrids of *P. grandiflorum*. They have larger flowers, which are always streaked or veined, and smaller green dentate leaves. There are further popular pelargoniums among the ivy-leaved or *P. peltatum* hybrids, which usually trail or hang down. Finally, there are many species pelargoniums with scented leaves, oak-leaf or ivy-leaf or miniature.

   Regal pelargoniums are usually 30–60 cm (1–2 ft) tall, and zonal pelargoniums the same, but the latter do need to be pruned as they can reach 2 m (6–7 ft). The scented-leaved ones are 30–90 cm (1–3 ft) tall, but again you can prune them to the height you want. (See p. 38 for some varieties worth looking out for.)

COMPOST Rich, loam-based.
TEMPERATURE Warm in summer; not above 10–15°C (50–59°F) in winter.
LIGHT A bright sunny place; though the *P. Peltatum* hybrids and scented-leaved species might prefer semi-shade.
WATER Generously in summer, sparingly in winter.
HUMIDITY Spray occasionally.
FEEDING Fortnightly April–September.
PROPAGATION From stem cuttings in spring or summer, or from seed in spring.
FLOWERING SEASON April–October.

PELLAEA ROTUNDIFOLIA · *Polypodiaceae* · Button Fern

An unusual fern in that it grows naturally in dry, rocky conditions. Pretty, with arching fronds of round, leathery leaflets. Height 20 cm (8 in).

COMPOST Peat-based.
TEMPERATURE Normal room; round about 12–16°C (54–61°F) in winter.
LIGHT Moderate; away from direct sun.
WATER Keep compost evenly moist throughout year, but a bit drier if the temperature is low in winter.
HUMIDITY Spray only when the temperature is above 16°C (61°F).
FEEDING Every 2 weeks May–September.
PROPAGATION Divide large plants in spring.

PEPEROMIA · *Piperaceae*

Small-scale clump-forming plants with fleshy leaves, many with very distinct markings. *P. argyreia* (*P. sandersii*) is one of the most beautiful, with silver and green leaves with bright green veins and red stems. *P. caperata* has deeply indented dark green leaves. Some species produce whitish-yellow 'rat's tail' flower spikes. Good for bottle gardens and plant cases. Height 20 cm (8 in).

COMPOST Peat-based in small pots.
TEMPERATURE Warm; not below 12–16°C (54–61°F) in winter.

LIGHT A north-facing window in summer; the same, or an east or west window, in winter.
WATER Best kept on the dry side; let compost dry out between waterings.
HUMIDITY High; spray frequently.
FEEDING Every 2 weeks April–September.
PROPAGATION From stem or leaf cuttings rooted at 18°C (64°F).

PHILODENDRON · *Araceae* · Sweetheart Vine

These are among the most popular and easy houseplants, erect shrubs and climbers from the rain forests of Central and South America. The commonest are *P. bipinnatifidum*, which has large, deeply incised leaves and grows to 1–2 m (3–7 ft), and *P. scandens* (the sweetheart vine), which climbs or trails almost indefinitely and has smaller heart-shaped leaves. *P. erubescens* and *P. elegans* are two other climbers worth trying. (See also p. 69.)

COMPOST Peat or loam.
TEMPERATURE Normal room; winter night minimum 14–16°C (57–61°F).
LIGHT Does best in a good light out of direct sun, but will tolerate a darkish position.
WATER Keep always moist in summer; water moderately in winter when the soil feels dry.
HUMIDITY High; spray daily with tepid water, or stand on moist pebbles or in damp peat and spray less frequently.
FEEDING Every 2 weeks April–September.
PROPAGATION From tip or stem cuttings, or from seed, in April or May (see p. 43).

PHOENIX · *Palmaceae* · Date Palm

Small spiky palms. *P. dactylifera* is the true, commercial date palm, relatively fast-growing for a palm. *P. canariensis* is still in nature a good-sized tree, but can be grown as a houseplant when young. *P. roebelinii* is a truly dwarf species, growing only to 60 cm–2 m (2–7 ft).

COMPOST Loam-based.
TEMPERATURE Normal to cool; winter night minimum 5°C (41°F).
LIGHT Moderate; probably some feet away from a window.
WATER Freely in summer, less in winter.
HUMIDITY Average; spray occasionally.
FEEDING Every 2–3 weeks April–August.
PROPAGATION Can sometimes be grown from a fresh date stone.

PHYLLITIS SCOLOPENDRIUM · *Aspleniaceae* · Hart's Tongue Fern

Ferns with single, strap-like, undivided fronds; some of the cultivars have frilled or crinkled edges. Fronds are 15–45 cm (6–18 in) long according to variety.

COMPOST Peat-based.
TEMPERATURE Average in summer; 14–16°C (57–61°F) in winter.
LIGHT A shady situation.
HUMIDITY High. Put pot on a tray of damp pebbles or in damp peat, and spray daily in warm conditions. Good in an enclosed plant case.
WATER Generously in summer; keep just moist in winter.
FEEDING Fortnightly April–August.
PROPAGATION By division of the roots around April.

PILEA · *Urticaceae* · Artillery Plant, Aluminium Plant

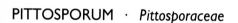

Small spreading plants with extremely decorative patterned leaves, quilted and silvery, bronze and copper-coloured. Growing only to 20–25 cm (8–10 in), they are ideal for bottle gardens and terrariums. One of the most popular species is *P. caderei*, the aluminium plant, with green leaves clearly marked in aluminium-grey.

COMPOST Peat-based.
TEMPERATURE 18–21°C (64–70°F) in summer; winter minimum 12–16°C (54–61°F). No draughts.
LIGHT Fairly low light, perhaps a metre or so away from a north- or east-facing window.
WATER Keep just moist in summer; water very little in winter.
HUMIDITY Doesn't need more than the occasional spray, but will do better if stood on moist pebbles or in damp peat and sprayed every few days in spring and summer.
FEEDING Every 2 weeks March–September.
PROPAGATION Tip cuttings taken in May root at 21°C (70°F).

PITTOSPORUM · *Pittosporaceae*

P. tobira is the best-known species for indoors, with shiny dark green leaves and clusters of fragrant pale yellow flowers in summer. Grows to 1 m (3 ft).

COMPOST Loam-based.
TEMPERATURE Cool; 4–8°C (39–46°F) in winter.
LIGHT As much as possible; full sun is fine. Put outside in summer if possible.
WATER Keep moist all the year round.
HUMIDITY Spray occasionally.
FEEDING Fortnightly April–August.
PROPAGATION From seed in spring, or from tip cuttings in summer.
FLOWERING SEASON April and May.

PLATYCERIUM · *Polypodiaceae* · Stag's Horn Fern

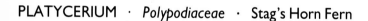

Epiphytic plants growing on branches of forest trees; the lower leaves are layered and shield-shaped, the upper are shaped like antlers. Usually grown on a log or a branch but will adapt to a pot. Fronds can grow up to 1 m (3 ft) in length.

COMPOST Peat mixed with sphagnum moss.
TEMPERATURE Warm in summer, 16–18°C (61–64°F) in winter if it is to carry on growing. It will survive but become dormant at 12°C (54°F).
LIGHT Good, but out of direct sun.
WATER Generously in the growing period, very sparingly in winter, using tepid water.
HUMIDITY Average to high; spray frequently.
FEEDING Once a month throughout the year as long as it isn't dormant.
PROPAGATION By pulling off the small plantlets which form on the roots, in March or April.

Poinsettia see **Euphorbia pulcherrima**.

POLYSTICHUM · *Polypodiaceae* · Polypody

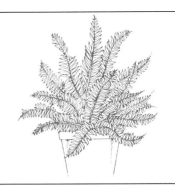

Ferns with wiry stems and finely divided fronds, usually about 30 cm (1 ft) tall.

COMPOST Loam-based.
TEMPERATURE Warm in summer; 12–16°C (54–61°F) in winter.
LIGHT Shade.
WATER Generously in summer, sparingly in winter.
HUMIDITY Spray frequently.
FEEDING Fortnightly April–August.
PROPAGATION By division of the rhizomes or from spores, in spring.

PRIMULA · *Primulaceae*

Temporary flowering pot plants for the winter; the two most popular are from China, *P. obconica*, with primrose-like flowers on 9 cm (3½ in) stems, and *P. malacoides* (30 cm/1 ft), with small star-like flowers in clusters. (See also p. 99.)

COMPOST Loam-based.
TEMPERATURE Cool; 12–16°C (54–61°F) – but flowers will last longer if it is around 12°C (54°F).
LIGHT As bright as possible; they will be alright in the sun as it is never too hot in winter.
WATER Keep just moist.
HUMIDITY Good kept on a tray of damp pebbles.
FEEDING Weekly while flowering.
PROPAGATION From seed annually in spring.
FLOWERING SEASON November–April.

PTERIS · *Pteridaceae or Polypodiaceae* · Brake, Ribbon Fern

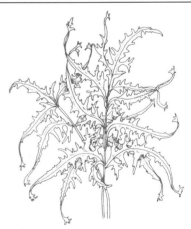

Many of these ferns are readily available and most make truly excellent houseplants; some, like *P. tremula*, have feathery fronds, and some, like the cultivars of *P. cretica*, have ribbon-like leaflets. Most are 45–50 cm (18–20 in) high, but *P. tremula* grows to 1–2 m (3–7 ft).

COMPOST Peat-based, quick-draining, with added grit.
TEMPERATURE Normal room in summer; in winter 12–16°C (54–61°F).
LIGHT A good light without direct sun is best, but they can survive in a fairly shady position.
WATER Keep constantly moist, not wet; give less in winter but do not let compost dry out.
HUMIDITY High, especially from April to August, or when the temperature exceeds 16°C (61°F). Spray daily, or stand pot on moist pebbles or in damp peat and spray less often.
FEEDING Every 2 weeks March–August.
PROPAGATION Divide the rhizomes in spring.

REBUTIA · Cactaceae

Miniature clump-forming cacti, covered in fine spines, which produce enormous flowers in a great variety of colours; ideal for window sills where space is short. Up to 8 cm (3 in) tall.

COMPOST Loam, free-draining with added grit.
TEMPERATURE Very warm in summer, cool in winter.
LIGHT Bright and sunny.
WATER Generously in summer, allowing to dry out almost completely between waterings; very little in winter.
HUMIDITY None; keep dry.
FEEDING Every 2–3 weeks April–September.
PROPAGATION From seed in spring.
FLOWERING SEASON June–August.
NOTE Lobivia is a very similar plant, to be cared for in exactly the same way.

REICHSTEINERIA · *Gesneriaceae* · Cardinal Flower

Tuberous-rooted perennials growing to 45 cm (18 in), with large, soft, velvety leaves and heads of bright pink or scarlet tubular flowers in summer and autumn. Usually bought in flower in May. Stems and leaves will wither after flowering; store root in dry peat in a cool place over the winter, and plant again in February or March.

COMPOST Peat or loam.
TEMPERATURE Cool and constant, and out of draughts. In winter keep the root in dry peat at 6°C (43°F).
LIGHT A good light, but out of direct sun.
WATER Keep moist while growing, dry in winter.
HUMIDITY High; spray frequently and stand on moist pebbles or in damp peat.
FEEDING Weekly with a weak solution, April–October.
PROPAGATION By division of the tubers, from basal cuttings taken in spring with a piece of the tuber attached, or from seed in spring.
FLOWERING SEASON May–August.

Rhapidophora aurea see **Scindapsus aureus.**

RHAPIS EXCELSA · *Palmaceae*

Dwarf palm with divided, leathery leaves and reed-like stems, growing to 1.2–2 m (4–7 ft) as a pot plant.

COMPOST Loam-based. ·
TEMPERATURE Warm in summer, cool in winter – 7°C (45°F).
LIGHT Good and bright, but out of direct sun.
WATER Generously in summer, sparingly in winter, but do not let compost dry out.
HUMIDITY Spray occasionally in summer.
FEEDING Fortnightly April–September.
PROPAGATION Not possible at home.

RHIPSALIDOPSIS · *Cactaceae* · Easter Cactus

Epiphytic cacti with flat, leaf-like, branching stems with red flowers in spring or early summer. Ideal for hanging pots or high shelves. Also known as *Schlumbergera gaertneri.* Stems up to about 1 m (3 ft) long.

COMPOST Rich. Leaf mould, loam and sharp sand, or a peat-based compost.
LIGHT A good light, out of direct sun in summer, though sun is alright in winter. Can go outside in a hanging basket in summer.
TEMPERATURE Warm in summer; 10–12°C (50–54°F) in winter.
WATER Generously in summer and autumn, sparingly in winter and spring, but do not let compost dry out.
HUMIDITY Average; spray occasionally.
FEEDING Every 2–3 weeks February–June.
PROPAGATION From cuttings of leaf segments, which root easily, in March or April.
FLOWERING SEASON March–May.

RHIPSALIS · *Cactaceae*

Strange-looking, branched, epiphytic cacti with clusters of angular branches. They bear pink or white flowers in summer followed by small white or red berries. 15–30 cm (6–12 in) height and spread.

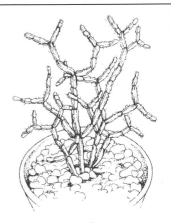

COMPOST Loam, peat and sharp sand, or special cactus mix.
TEMPERATURE Warm all the year round; winter night minimum 7–10°C (45–50°F).
LIGHT Semi-shade.
WATER Keep moist all the year.
HUMIDITY Spray occasionally in summer.
FEEDING Every 2–3 weeks April–August.
PROPAGATION From stem cuttings or from seed, in April or May.
FLOWERING SEASON July and August.

ROSA CHINENSIS VAR. MINIMA · *Rosaceae* · Miniature Rose

Miniature roses, many of which are varieties of *R. chinensis*, are round about 10–25 cm (4–10 in) high, according to variety, with pink, red, white or yellow flowers to scale. They are exactly like their big brothers outside. They do best outdoors in a window box or pot but can survive well either as permanent or temporary houseplants as long as they are in a well-ventilated place. The little plants must be gently pruned in spring, and all dead flowers must be removed to extend the flowering season. (See also p. 54.)

COMPOST Loam-based.
TEMPERATURE Moderate; cool in winter, 6–8°C (43–46°F).
LIGHT Bright, but shaded from the hottest sun; an east or west window is ideal.
WATER Moderately in the growing season, from April to October; very little after flowering.
HUMIDITY Spray frequently and stand pots on damp pebbles in summer, or in a warm room.
FEEDING Fortnightly April–October.
PROPAGATION Not possible in the home.
FLOWERING SEASON June–October.

SANSEVIERIA · *Liliaceae* · Mother-in-Law's Tongue

Succulents from tropical Africa, among the easiest and most tolerant of houseplants, even surviving neglect, shade and cold; they only dislike temperatures below 10–15°C (50–59°F) and overwatering. The upright, fleshy, stemless leaves are sword-shaped with lateral markings. Up to 1.5 m (5 ft).

COMPOST Loam- or peat-based, with added grit.
TEMPERATURE Normal room or up to 26°C (79°F) in summer; minimum in winter 10–15°C (50–59°F).
LIGHT Almost any, shade or sun.
WATER Sparingly; water only when the compost is dry, and hardly at all in winter. Never leave water in the saucer.
HUMIDITY Hardly necessary; in very dry conditions spray occasionally.
FEEDING Not necessary.
PROPAGATION Green forms by rooting 8 cm (3 in) leaf sections; yellow-edged forms by division of the roots. May is the ideal time.

SAXIFRAGA STOLONIFERA · *Saxifragaceae* · Mother of Thousands

A trailing plant with thin stems 45 cm (18 in) long with young plantlets at the ends. The small starry white flowers appear in summer. The variety 'Tricolor' has variegated leaves and is the best for average room cultivation.

COMPOST Loam-based.
TEMPERATURE Cool; 8–12°C (46–54°F) in winter.

LIGHT It likes a very good light, shaded only from the hottest summer sun, but tolerates some shade.
WATER Keep moist from spring to autumn; water more sparingly over the winter when it is resting.
HUMIDITY Spray occasionally.
FEEDING Fortnightly in the growing season, April–August.
PROPAGATION Easy; separate the plantlets from the parent plant in summer, and pot in groups of three.
FLOWERING SEASON June–August.

SCHEFFLERA ACTINOPHYLLA · *Araliaceae* · Umbrella Tree

Imposing and fast-growing plants, with large palmate leaves, they can reach small tree proportions, up to 2 m (7 ft).

COMPOST Peat- or loam-based.
TEMPERATURE Normal room; not below 12°C (54°F) in winter, 16–18°C (61–64°F) is ideal.
LIGHT Moderate; does not mind low light.
WATER Keep just moist in spring and summer; water more sparingly autumn and winter.
HUMIDITY Spray frequently in warm, dry conditions.
FEEDING Every 2–3 weeks April–September for large, established plants, every week for young plants.
PROPAGATION From seed in spring at 21°C (70°F) (see p. 43).

SCHLUMBERGERA TRUNCATA · *Cactaceae* · Christmas Cactus

Also sold as zygocactus, these are easily grown forest leaf cacti, excellent for trailing from baskets or high places, with brilliant red or purple flowers in winter. Stems are 30–45 cm (12–18 in) long. (See also p. 93.) *S. gaertneri* is the Easter cactus (see **Rhipsalidopsis**).

COMPOST Peat-based with added sand or grit.
TEMPERATURE 12–16°C (54–61°F) is ideal when flowering, though it will tolerate warmer; as cool as possible in summer.
LIGHT Bright; out of direct sun in summer.
WATER Average, but allow to dry out almost completely between waterings. After flowering stop watering except for an occasional drop and keep cool for 2 months.
HUMIDITY Stand pot on moist pebbles or in damp peat, and spray occasionally in warm conditions.
FEEDING Every week from late summer to late autumn.
PROPAGATION From leaf segments, which root easily in summer.
FLOWERING SEASON November–February.

SCINDAPSUS AUREUS · *Araceae* · Devil's Ivy, Pothos

Easily grown climbing plants, relatives of the philodendrons, their glossy, heart-shaped leaves often streaked with yellow and white; they also trail elegantly. Grows to 2 m (7 ft). Also sold under the name *Rhaphidophora aurea*.

COMPOST Peat-based.
TEMPERATURE Ordinary room; not below 16°C (61°F) in winter.
LIGHT Fairly low light for green-leaved varieties, brighter for variegated ones; never in direct sun.
WATER Keep just moist in spring and summer; water sparingly in winter.
HUMIDITY High; spray frequently, or stand on trays of damp pebbles or in peat and spray less often.
FEEDING Every 2–3 weeks April–August for large, mature plants, weekly for young plants.
PROPAGATION From 8–10 cm (3–4 in) tip cuttings, rooted in sand at 21°C (70°F) in summer.

SEDUM · *Crassulaceae* · Stonecrop

The houseplant members of this family of succulents are troublefree little plants with fleshy leaves; some trail, like *S. sieboldii*, and some are bushy, like *S. griseum*. Height 20 cm (8 in).

COMPOST Loam-based with extra grit.
TEMPERATURE Very warm in summer, cool in winter.
LIGHT Bright and sunny.
WATER Water well in summer, hardly at all in winter.
HUMIDITY Not necessary; keep dry.
FEEDING Every 2–3 weeks April–August.
PROPAGATION Easily rooted from cuttings and pieces between April and June.

SELAGINELLA · *Selaginellaceae* · Creeping Moss

Tiny creeping plants akin to ferns, ideal for bottle gardens. Height 10–30 cm (4–12 in).

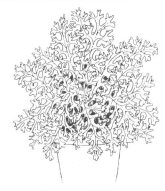

COMPOST Peat-based.
TEMPERATURE Warm in summer, 14–16°C (57–61°F) in winter.
LIGHT Shade.
WATER Generously in summer; slightly less in winter.
HUMIDITY Very high. Stand on moist pebbles or in damp peat and spray frequently if not in a terrarium.
FEEDING Fortnightly April–August.
PROPAGATION By division or from cuttings in spring.

SETCREASEA · *Commelinaceae*

S. purpurea is one of the best purple-blue plants; it tends to grow horizontally, and trail. It is a relative of tradescantia. Stems 30–45 cm (12–18 in). (See also p. 46.)

COMPOST Peat-based.
TEMPERATURE Normal room in summer, cool in winter.
LIGHT Bright and sunny.
WATER Keep always moist, but be careful as water tends to mark the leaves.
HUMIDITY Hardly necessary.
FEEDING Every 2–3 weeks April–August.
PROPAGATION Stem cuttings root very quickly and easily, April–July. If you just snap a piece off it will root.

SINNINGIA · *Gesneriaceae* · Gloxinia

Tuberous-rooted flowering plants with brilliantly coloured trumpet flowers and furry leaves. The flowers come in white and many shades of purple, red, pink and mauve, some edged with white. The tubers can be stored in dry peat for another year and brought into growth again some time between late January and March. Up to 30 cm (1 ft) tall. (See also p. 11.)

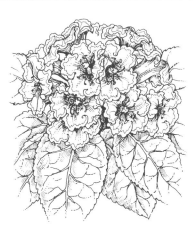

COMPOST Peat-based, the tuber tops level with the soil surface.
TEMPERATURE Normal room in summer; winter minimum 16°C (61°F). Keep cool while tuber is stored in peat.
LIGHT Bright, but not in direct sun.
WATER Keep moist but never soggy; reduce watering when the flowers fade and stop when the leaves die.
HUMIDITY Ideally stand the pots on moist pebbles or in peat. Spray foliage in hot weather but not the flowers, as water will mark them.
FEEDING Every 2 weeks when growing and flowering.
PROPAGATION You could try leaf cuttings in summer; they will usually root at 21°C (70°F) in a propagator.
FLOWERING SEASON June–September.

SOLANUM · *Solanaceae* · Jerusalem Cherry, Winter Cherry

These temporary houseplants, relatives both of the deadly nightshade and of the potato, are usually sold in the winter and only kept while their bright berries or fruits last. *S. capsicastrum* is the winter cherry, *S. pseudocapsicum* the Jerusalem cherry. But if you do want to keep them for a second year they can be cut back in February and repotted; from May until September they are best put out of doors. Height 30–60 cm (1–2 ft).

COMPOST They stay in the pots they are bought in. Loam-based if you keep them for another year and repot.
TEMPERATURE Cool; 10°C (50°F) is ideal in winter; put outside in summer.
LIGHT The brightest possible, in or out of sun.
WATER Keep always moist with regular watering.
FEEDING Not necessary if treating plants as disposable. If you want to try to keep a plant for a second year feed fortnightly April–August.
HUMIDITY Spray daily.
PROPAGATION From seed in spring.
FLOWERING SEASON Fruits October–February.

SONERILA · *Melastomataceae*

Small neat shrubs with sumptuous silver-patterned leaves, ideal for bottle gardens. Usually available only from specialist nurseries. Height 15 cm (6 in).

COMPOST Peat-based, in a terrarium, or in small, shallow pans 10 cm (4 in) wide.
TEMPERATURE Around 21–24°C (70–75°F); no lower than 18°C (64°F) in winter.
LIGHT Shady in summer – the shade of larger plants is ideal; slightly brighter in winter.
WATER Keep moist at all times; give slightly less water in winter.
HUMIDITY High; moist warmth is essential. Spray daily and stand on moist pebbles or in damp peat if not in a terrarium.
FEEDING Fortnightly April–August.
PROPAGATION From 8 cm (3 in) basal cuttings in spring.

SPARMANNIA AFRICANA · *Tiliaceae* · House Lime, African Hemp

A fast-growing evergreen shrub or tree with large, apple-green, furry leaves and white gold-fringed flowers in spring. Usually cut back in April. 1–2 m (3–7 ft).

COMPOST Loam-based.
TEMPERATURE Cool to normal; 6–10°C (43–50°F) in winter.
LIGHT A well-ventilated, sunny place, but out of the hottest sun in summer.
WATER Water freely in spring and summer, more sparingly in winter.
HUMIDITY Spray occasionally.
FEEDING Every 2–3 weeks March–August.
PROPAGATION Stem cuttings root easily at 18–21°C (64–70°F) in March or April.
FLOWERING SEASON January–March.

SPATHIPHYLLUM WALLISII · *Araceae* · White Flag

Plants of the arum family with white flowers consisting of a finely pointed spathe and central spadix, 30–40 cm (12–16 in) tall. Some hybrids flower throughout the year.

COMPOST Loam-based.
TEMPERATURE Normal room; 16–18°C (61–64°F) is ideal in winter, and not below 12°C (54°F).
LIGHT A shady place, well out of the sun.
WATER Keep moist in summer; water more sparingly in winter.
HUMIDITY High; spray daily and stand pot on damp pebbles or in moist peat. The plant is very sensitive to dry air in summer.

FEEDING Fortnightly April–September.
PROPAGATION Divide established clumps in April or May.
FLOWERING SEASON April–August.

STEPHANOTIS FLORIBUNDA · *Asclepiadaceae* · Madagascar Jasmine

A climbing shrub with glossy dark green leaves and white, star-shaped, fragrant flowers, reaching 3 m (10 ft) in a conservatory but happy trained on canes or bent wire as a houseplant. Do not move it about or turn it as this will make the flower buds drop.

COMPOST Loam-based.
TEMPERATURE Warm in summer, 12–14°C (54–57°F) in winter. The plant likes a well-ventilated position.
LIGHT Keep out of direct sun in summer; otherwise give as much light as possible.
WATER Freely in spring and summer; less from autumn on, but do not allow the soil ball to dry out. Use tepid soft water.
HUMIDITY Stand pot on moist pebbles or in damp peat throughout the year, and spray frequently in early summer.
FEEDING Fortnightly April–October.
PROPAGATION From cuttings of non-flowering side-shoots in early summer.
FLOWERING SEASON May–October.

STRELITZIA REGINAE · *Musaceae* · Bird of Paradise Flower

An evergreen perennial with extraordinary flowers like birds' heads with beak-shaped bracts and blue and orange flowers, growing to 1–1.5 m (3–5 ft).

COMPOST Loam-based.
TEMPERATURE Warm in summer, 10°C (50°F) in winter.
LIGHT Very well lit but shaded from the hottest summer sun. Likes being put outside on good days in summer.
WATER Freely in spring and summer; keep almost dry in winter.
HUMIDITY Spray occasionally.
FEEDING Fortnightly May–September.
PROPAGATION From seed or by division of the roots in spring. Seed sown in January or February at 18°C (64°F) may produce flowers in the autumn; seed sown in March or April will produce flowers the following summer.
FLOWERING SEASON April and May.

STREPTOCARPUS · *Gesneriaceae* · Cape Primrose

Soft green primula-like leaves and clusters of trumpet-shaped flowers of white, pink, red and blue, 25 cm (10 in) tall. Like their relatives the African violets they grow well for some people and not at all for others.

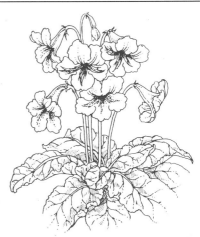

COMPOST Loam- or peat-based.
TEMPERATURE Warm; 18–20°C (64–68°F) in winter. Well-ventilated.
LIGHT A good light, but away from direct sun.
WATER Generously in summer, sparingly in winter; the cooler the room the less water is needed.
HUMIDITY High; stand pots on damp pebbles or moist peat and spray frequently.
FEEDING Fortnightly March–September.
PROPAGATION From seed at 18°C (64°F), from 8 cm (3 in) leaf cuttings rooted in damp sand at 21°C (70°F) in summer, or by dividing clumps in spring or early summer. Sow seed in January or February for autumn flowers, in March or April for summer flowers the following year.
FLOWERING SEASON May–October, sometimes even longer.

SYNGONIUM · *Araceae*

Trailing or climbing plants related to the philodendrons, with shiny arrow-shaped leaves, which divide into three, five or even eight leaflets when mature. Grows to 1.2–1.5 m (4–5 ft).

COMPOST Loam-based.
TEMPERATURE Warm; not below 15°C (59°F) in winter.
LIGHT Good, but out of direct sun.
WATER Freely in summer, sparingly in winter.
HUMIDITY High; place pot in moist peat or on damp gravel or pebbles, and spray frequently in summer or if the room is warm and dry.
FEEDING Fortnightly April–August.
PROPAGATION From stem tip cuttings in summer.

TILLANDSIA CYANEA · *Bromeliaceae*

An attractive bromeliad from Central and South America, *T. cyanea* has arching, grass-like leaves and a sheaf of pink bracts with violet flowers. Most successful in a heated plant window, terrarium or greenhouse. Height 30–60 cm (1–2 ft).

COMPOST Peat, sand and sphagnum moss.
TEMPERATURE Warm throughout year; soil and air temperature of 18–20°C (64–68°F).
LIGHT A good light, but out of direct sun.
WATER Keep always moist with soft, tepid water.
HUMIDITY High; stand on moist pebbles or in damp peat and spray frequently if not in a plant window or terrarium.
FEEDING Fortnightly April–August.
PROPAGATION From offsets from the parent plant in spring and summer.
FLOWERING SEASON It usually flowers in summer.

TRADESCANTIA · *Commelinaceae* · Wandering Jew

Popular creeping and trailing plants for hanging baskets and pots. *T. fluminensis* 'Variegata' and *T.f.* 'Quicksilver' have pointed green and white striped leaves. Stems up to 1 m (3 ft).

COMPOST Peat- or loam-based.
TEMPERATURE Normal living room; not below 10°C (50°F) in winter.
LIGHT Bright and sunny.
WATER Generously in summer, less in winter.
HUMIDITY Mist-spray frequently.
FEEDING Monthly April–September.
PROPAGATION Stem cuttings root easily in water and can be potted at any time.
NOTE Zebrina is a very similar plant, to be cared for in exactly the same way.

VRIESIA SPLENDENS · *Bromeliaceae* · Flaming Sword

Dramatic bromeliad from South America, with a rosette of arching, strap-like leaves banded in brown or purple. From this rises a 45 cm (18 in) flower spike, with brilliant red bracts lightly touched with yellow – hence its common name, flaming sword. Best in a greenhouse, heated plant window, or terrarium, but the newer hybrids are much more tolerant of ordinary room conditions than the older varieties.

COMPOST Peat, sand and spaghnum moss.
TEMPERATURE Warm; soil and air temperature of 18–20°C (64–68°F).
LIGHT A good light but out of direct sun.
WATER Keep compost moist, using soft, tepid water. Keep the central cup of the rosette filled with water.
HUMIDITY High; stand on moist pebbles or in damp peat and spray frequently if not in a plant window or terrarium.

FEEDING Fortnightly April–August.
PROPAGATION From offsets in spring and summer.
FLOWERING SEASON Can produce a flower spike at any time of year, but usually in summer.

YUCCA · *Liliaceae*

Y. aloifolia has a scaly stem and spiky leaf clusters 45–60 cm (18–24 in) long, and will grow to 1.2–2 m (4–7 ft) as a pot plant.

COMPOST Loam-based.
TEMPERATURE Cool; 6°C (43°F) in winter; outside if possible in summer.
LIGHT Bright and sunny, especially in winter.
WATER Generously in summer, draining well; keep almost dry in winter.
HUMIDITY Keep on the dry side, spraying very occasionally.
FEEDING Fortnightly April–September.
PROPAGATION Not possible in the home.

ZANTEDESCHIA · *Araceae* · Arum, Calla or Trumpet Lily

Lilies with spear-shaped leaves and trumpet-shaped spathes of white or yellow in spring and summer. 60 cm–1.5 m (2–5 ft).

COMPOST Peat-based.
TEMPERATURE Warm in summer; cool (8–12°C/46–54°F) in winter.
LIGHT A good light, but out of direct sun. Ideally outside in spring and summer.
WATER Freely in the growing period; keep dry after flowering and gradually increase water from January or February onwards.
HUMIDITY Spray occasionally in summer.
FEEDING Fortnightly March–August.
PROPAGATION By removing offsets in January or February, or by dividing the rhizomes when replanting in the spring.
FLOWERING SEASON March–June.

Zygocactus see **Schlumbergera truncata.**

Index

Page numbers in *italics* refer to colour illustrations